THERE'S
SIMON GARNER

An Autobiography

The Parrs Wood Press
MANCHESTER

First Published 2002

THE PARRS WOOD PRESS
St Wilfrid's Enterprise Centre
Royce Road, Manchester, M15 5BJ
www.parrswoodpress.com

© Simon Garner & Richard Slater 2002

ISBN: 1 903158 36 2

Cover art and design by David Fagan

Printed by:
MFP Design and Print
Longford Trading Estate
Thomas Street
Stretford
Manchester M32 0JT

To the memory of my mum and dad

Acknowledgements

Thanks are due to many and apologies to those not mentioned.

The late Peter White provided access to comprehensive Blackburn Rovers playing records as well as plenty of encouragement. The Lancashire Evening Telegraph and, in particular, their librarians Charmaine and Val, allowed us to rummage through their vast collection of pictures and cuttings. The Electric Chairboys gave us some excellent background information. Ann Collins diligently typed seemingly endless interview material. Paul Dennis supplied photographs from the Wycombe era. Chris O'Donnell provided the inspiration for the book after a chance meeting with SG. Andrew Searle of The Parrs Wood Press was flexible over deadlines. Seamus Heffernan loaned us a variety of publications from his collection. Tim Aldred proof-read and made valuable suggestions. Several former players and managers were happy to be interviewed. Kenny Dalglish enthusiastically provided the foreword. And our families let us get on with it when the washing-up needed doing.

Picture credits

The cover shots and many of those within these pages are courtesy of the Lancashire Evening Telegraph. Other pictures are courtesy of Paul Dennis and private collections.

.

Simon Garner and Richard Slater, July 2002

Contents

Foreword

By Kenny Dalglish

What stood out about Simon throughout his career was his finishing ability. He was a very natural striker with two good feet and he anticipated the game very well. He was never that quick - there wouldn't be much in it in a race between me and him - but he had it upstairs and knew where the goal was.

Simon was a tremendous servant to Blackburn and a very fine player, but football was changing in the early '90s when I went to the club. He was never exactly the most disciplined of players - he liked a drink and a smoke and I was never going to be able to change his ways - but that approach to the game was on the way out. Players were becoming increasingly conscious of how they should look after themselves.

Maybe he would have played at a higher level if he had kicked the booze and fags into touch, but I'm not so sure. The way he lived his life probably helped him. He is what he is and lived his life the way he wanted to by enjoying himself on and off the pitch.

When I arrived at Blackburn, Simon was coming towards the end of his career and he knew he wasn't going to see much first team action with the changes that were happening at the club, but he responded well and played an important lesser role as the season went on.

When it came to the play-off final at Wembley in 1992, the club was allowed three non-playing team members to sit on the bench with the staff and substitutes.

The only place for Simon to be that day was with the team. He had given so much to the club and this was one of the most important days in its recent history.

Like Tony Parkes, who I asked to lead out the team, Simon was part of the fabric of the club and had helped create the platform for us to build on. His role had been a crucial one.

He never won much during a lean time at the club but he had been a magnificent servant and I know how much it meant to him to be with the team that day - if you look at the celebration pictures, they say it all.

PREFACE

Spring 2000

Hertford 0 Flackwell Heath 1

There's ten minutes to go. I'm knackered and happy to be substituted.

We, that's Flackwell Heath, are leading Hertford 1-0 but since both sides are mid-table in Ryman League Division Three, the outcome counts for little.

A couple of Blackburn Rovers fans are there to watch and cheer me on. It happens every so often and it means a lot that even now, nearly a decade after leaving Ewood Park, people are still interested in me. It's not difficult to spot them because the attendance today is only about seventy.

One of the lads is smoking which is good news because my fags are in the dressing room. So I watch the remainder of the game with them on the touchline and cadge cigarettes.

They talk about the game and want to know what I'm up to. All fairly harmless stuff and I enjoy their company. We arrange to meet for a pint after the game but a mix-up means it doesn't happen.

My back is aching and my knees sound like a milkshake machine - the occasional rattle, the odd squelch.

I haven't trained this week, and that's become a normal routine. Contrary to popular belief, I always liked training. But I'm forty and my body's reached the point where it can only take one bout of serious punishment each week, and even that's starting to become a strain.

I still love playing, though. Why else would I play at this level? Perhaps I should explain exactly what level this is. It's a step or two below Accrington Stanley and a step or two above pub football.

The league has a fair smattering of ex-pros and Graham Roberts, who used to play for Spurs and Rangers, is the player-manager at Hertford. Today he's been in goal, and I haven't beaten him.

I'm starting to think my Saturdays could be better spent doing something else.

It's different for the youngsters around me. Some of them still have dreams about playing professionally. For the vast majority it won't ever happen, but they should keep dreaming.

My dreams were to break goal-scoring records, play at Wembley and perform at the highest level of English football.

1

LEARNING
1959 to 1976

I WAS BORN AT NANNY GARNER'S. November 23, 1959 at Fishtoft, near Boston, some time between Ten and midnight. Dad was a lorry driver and away working so he missed it. When he was out of town, mum would sometimes stay at her mother-in-law's and when she was heavily pregnant with me, it was insisted on. There was never any question of me being born in the hospital. The reason I know the time is because Dad left my uncle Ivor the name of the club he'd be in that night and he learned about his second son's arrival in a strange town with a bingo card in one hand, a fag in the other and a glass of lemon and lime in front of him. He didn't drink, but he did like bingo!

Some think it's in the genes. A parent, brother or cousin - a distant uncle perhaps - must have been involved at some level of sport, and that sparks a domino effect of achievement through successive generations. Not in my family. The highest sporting honour belonged to my dad - and he was a second-rate goalkeeper in a third-rate team in a fourth-rate amateur league. No-one was any good at sport. Only me. Just as well too, because I was never much good at anything else.

If sporting ability doesn't necessarily pass through the generations, perhaps it's a sporting obsession which is transferred. You know the situation - the offspring is transfixed by the bright lights and heady atmosphere of a major sporting event. And once tasted, the ambition is inspired and the obsession reborn.

Nope. Not me. I was brought up in Boston, Lincolnshire, and it's not what you'd call a hot-bed of sporting prowess. The nearest football club was Lincoln City and, in the flesh, I saw just one professional game before signing apprentice terms with Blackburn Rovers. It was a night match at the City Ground, Nottingham. I have no idea who Forest were playing and I can't remember the score but I know I was bored. I wanted to be playing footie with my mates.

I never was much of a spectator and I'm still not, though I do some matchday public relations work for Wycombe Wanderers. There is simply no substitute for kicking a ball around. I'm forty-two years old. I played professionally for twenty years and only now, after one too many kicks in the calf, have I decided it's time to pack it all in, give or take the odd 5-a-side or veterans game. I played until the summer of 2000. I'd play with anyone, for anyone. Money had nothing to do with it.

In fairness to my dad, Geoff, he wasn't such a bad player - or so he always told me - but his cartilages packed in. He was a big sports fan, much more than I could ever be. I think it was because his own ambitions were frustrated by a lack of, well, ability, that he became a once-removed sports addict. He would watch any kind of sport at whatever level and whenever he could. It could be schoolboys playing cricket or it could be some obscure Olympic event on the box - if it was available, he'd be watching.

Football was his favourite though, and I know he'd like to have watched much more but Boston is miles from anywhere. Boston United were a quality side, the Rushden and Diamonds of the '70s, but for professional football it was Lincoln City or Forest. In my late teens it was the Brian Clough era, though when they started to romp their way round Europe I was at Blackburn and my dad was more interested in my career than watching anyone else. He never really had allegiance to any particular team, just to watch was the joy of the game for him and he didn't need to be wearing a scarf to prove he was a real fan.

I'm sure that's why he became interested in coaching. It was only at an amateur level, but dad got quite involved with a number of teams. He was ambitious for his players, though not in that over-bearing way some parents want their children to live out their own unfulfilled dreams. He just wanted to see more kids involved in sport rather than have them hanging around getting into trouble.

David, my brother, is seven years older than me and was never remotely interested in sport when he was younger. All I can remember about him when we were little was that he was mad about model aeroplanes. I could never work it out, to be honest. What was the point in sitting indoors with a tube of glue, 200 bits of grey plastic and an instruction leaflet which read like it had been written by the bloke who sweeps up the factory? What was wrong with going out, kicking a ball, playing a bit of cricket, going swimming? He improved with age though, and he did play for my dad's team when he got older, but he was never really any good. But he was more academic than me and he definitely cared more for his future. David seemed to have sensible plans while all I wanted was to be playing football professionally. As I've matured, so has my outlook on life. I can now look as far forward as tomorrow, but not much further.

It served him well too. He went on to university which was as big a deal in my family as me playing my debut for Blackburn. It was different thirty years ago, not as many people went to university and certainly not many from working-class council estates in Boston. Dad was a driver and mum was a hairdresser who later worked in a bakery and a dress shop, so David's achievement was a source of genuine pride to them. He teaches Art and Design now, which perhaps explains why he was so obsessive about getting exactly the right colours in those stupid little tin pots to finish off his replica Spitfires or whatever they were. Still, he made a career out of something he always liked doing. And it'll take him through to retirement on a decent wage. The irony, by the way, isn't lost on me - I've been largely scraping a living as a painter and decorator for the past few years.

We were never close, but that's not to say we've not always been friends - we have - and, with the exception of my dad, he followed my career as keenly as anyone. But when we were younger we had nothing in common and with seven years between us we had a wholly different set of friends. When I started primary school he was moving into secondary school. When I went to secondary school he left home for university. And when I moved to Blackburn he was taking his first steps into teaching.

I've never considered myself academic because I was always side-tracked by sport, but I did manage to pass my 11-plus and was accepted into Boston Grammar School. So there must have been something there. There was never any pressure on me though. The achievement was that I'd got there and I'd always told mum and dad I was going to be a footballer and they never once tried to persuade me otherwise.

School was good. I liked it. Not the lessons, of course, I was never much use in class, but school gave me a chance to play more sports. After school I'd get home, throw my bag inside and play football or cricket with the lads in the street.

LEARNING

And at school, they made it all a bit more formal. I learnt how to play tennis and the cricket coaching was excellent - I had county trials but never made the team. I wasn't bothered at all, only football counted.

It was a great childhood, and I was allowed to grow up just as I wanted to. I did what I wanted, within reason, and my parents were always supportive. Clifton Road, Fishtoft, was where we lived. We had the top flat in a two-storey house with two bedrooms for the four of us. It was never warm - you had hot and you had cold. Mostly cold. There were coal fires in the kitchen and the living room and no central heating. I'd get out of bed and it was freezing. I'd have to run to the kitchen and sit in front of the fire just to get dressed without contracting hypothermia.

What I really liked about living there was the fact it was on the estate. I've been living in my house in Cookham, Berkshire, for three years now and I hardly know any of my neighbours. I know some of the crowd down the pub, of course, but not that well and I don't think there's anyone in the area who knows what I used to do for a living. But on the estate I knew everybody and, on Clifton Road, I knew everybody very well. Outside the house was a big green. That sounds a bit posh, and it wasn't, but it was a great big grass area. The Wembley of Fishtoft. Or something. Dad's brothers lived close by and a lot of people who worked at my dad's firm lived on the estate. I don't want to sound all sentimental, and I know it's all a horrible cliché, but you could leave your doors unlocked and let kids play out till it was dark. And that's what we used to do.

Dad never worked weekends at all, which was great. When I was very young we'd watch local football on a Saturday afternoon, we'd be in the baths for 7.30 on Sundays and in the afternoons it'd be back to the parks for more football. He was often away for three or four nights during the week with his job, so his weekends were special to him. But they always revolved around watching or playing sport. It was the same with holidays. We'd meet up with other families so there'd be maybe twenty or thirty of us and it was always football, cricket, tennis, swimming. Anything so long as there was sport involved.

I'd be about ten when he started coaching. He took on two teams, Boston Colts under-16s and under-18s. I've no idea how it all began but he knew a lot from his own playing days and there was no-one in Lincolnshire who'd seen more football than my dad. He'd obviously learnt a lot too, because his teams were incredibly successful - within a couple of years they were winning the league every year and they were always in with a shout of the cups. He managed to attract the best young players around and made them one of the hottest teams in the county.

The first match I remember playing in was for his under-16 side. I was twelve. If he ever had a problem with his teams it was that some of the older players started to become attracted to the snooker halls, the pubs and the girls. So occasionally there were gaps on the pitch, despite the fact we'd trawl players' houses on a Sunday morning looking for stragglers. By this point we were also at the football ground two nights a week getting the pitch ready for the first team. Mum was fine about all this. She was a generous, loving woman and was just happy for my dad to be enjoying himself. I was living and breathing football from then on. I knew all the teams, all the players. I wasn't as obsessive as my dad, though my collection of magazines and cards was growing nicely. If I'd had doubts before, I knew now there was only one thing I was ever going to do when I finished school. The game, the first I remember, was a Lincolnshire Cup Final. We were a player short and dad decided it was time I tested myself against bigger, stronger, meaner boys. Actually he was desperate and I had my boots on. I scored and we won. Mum was proud as punch of both of us.

I don't want to give the impression that somehow mum was left out with dad and me being so close. It wasn't like that. And it wasn't just my dad who worked hard in that house. When mum worked at the bakery, I'd jump on the back of her bike and she'd cycle to Nanny Garner's where I'd stay until it was time to go to school. As soon as the last bell went, she was at the gates, we'd go home, I'd play out and she'd do the housework. And dad would be on the other side of the country lugging his lorry round. When I got older I'd bike it myself, but the draw of Nanny Garner's never changed. I had one school dinner and that was it. I didn't like it. So every lunchtime I'd get back on the bike and cycle to her house. It was a two-mile round trip which, in the freezing cold depths of a Lincolnshire winter, could be a trial. She'd make me bread and gravy or pancakes, egg and chips. When I was older, she'd slip me twenty fags from her pension money.

In Boston there was a choice of two schools, or three if you count St Bede's. But nobody went to St Bede's. Unless you were a Catholic. The other choice was Kitwood. Academia was never my strong point and I'm not sure I could spell the word without the aid of a dictionary. But I wasn't daft and I knew the Grammar School, being a Grammar School, had better sports facilities. With this insider knowledge, the 11-plus was never going to be anything more than a formality. Unfortunately, once I was in the schoolwork took a tumble. But the football was terrific. By the time I was fourteen I was only interested in games lessons and sports matches. The crowning achievement was being selected to play for the school's first-team - the school had a sixth form. Not only was I playing with lads - men - four years older than me and not only was I the youngest player to ever get into that team but, best of all, I got to miss double history every Wednesday afternoon for matches. It was brilliant - you could see my classroom from the pitch. It was inevitable my schoolwork would suffer, and it did. The facilities were fantastic and I was playing tennis and basketball and I was in the swimming and cricket teams. Strangely, rugby wasn't played. I was pleased about that. I didn't like the game.

Rod Dunn was my sports master and he was superb. He persuaded me to go to county cricket trials and suggested I put myself forward as a wicket-keeper. I ignored the advice, went as a fielder and bowler and never got past the first selection round. I wasn't disappointed at all. In fact, I deliberately contributed to my own failure. When he was telling me I should go, I told him I was really only interested in football.

"You're a good footballer, Simon, but you're a good cricketer too - you could perhaps make a living in both of them."

Well hang on a minute, Dunny. Thanks for the flattery, but let's get some perspective here. The end of the cricket season overlaps the start of the football season. End of story. Mr Dunn never fell out with me though, he knew what I really wanted. Unlike Philip Johnson. A man, I am ashamed to admit, that I detest. He was the headmaster and, by an unfortunate twist of bad fate, he later became headmaster at Queen Elizabeth Grammar School in Blackburn. Just to be in the same town as him was enough to make me feel queasy. I got my own back though. Twice. When I joined Blackburn he had no option but to see me regularly plastered over the pages of the local papers. And I think even he would have to have conceded that I'd done alright. The first piece of revenge came much earlier.

I'd always swum and for a time I was a member of Boston Swimming Club which the school seemed to think made me something of a butterfly expert. Granted, I'd once swum a competitive length for the school in our own pool. It was 15 metres long and I just about managed to reach the other end without drowning. The next time I was picked was for some inter-school event - off home ground. The pool was 25 metres long and by half-way I was sinking. I hated it.

I happened to be ill on the day of the next gala. I really was ill and it was no fun - mum and dad were both at work, Nanny Garner must have been busy, and I was miserable. I knew it was serious, because I couldn't even muster the energy for a kickabout. The phone rang. It was on the floor below.

"Hello?"

"Where are you Garner?"

"I'm ill sir"

"You're skiving, more like. You're a disgrace."

Not for the first time, nor the last, Johnson got it wrong. Then he made a very bad mistake. He rang my dad at work. I only have his side of the story, but it went something like this:

"Mr Garner, this is Simon's headmaster. I'm appalled your son is skipping school just to avoid a length of butterfly."

Now dad, being a lorry driver, knew one or two choice phrases, and Johnson got them full-on. He even wrote to Johnson, the only letter I ever remember him writing. It was littered with F-words. I don't remember us getting a reply. No matter, I never swam for the school again.

THERE'S ONLY ONE SIMON GARNER

I could never really work Johnson out. I remember him telling me I was just wasting my time, that I should stop thinking I could ever kick a ball around for money. It seemed such a stupid way to deal with a child's ambitions. It wasn't as if he was trying to get me to spread my energies, he just told me I should be thinking of my future, of responsibilities, of getting a proper job, of stopping playing football. I could never understand his attitude. Schools like BGS and QEGS are renowned not just for the academic side of things but for sport as well. And he just didn't seem to like sport at all, other than to occasionally bask in the reflected glory of Mr Dunn and the occasional big victory for one of the teams.

I suppose breaking into the first team when I was fourteen was when I started to think I really had a chance of making it. The local football scene in Boston was very tightly-knit and well connected with the professional game, certainly at scouting level. I was also playing for dad's teams and it didn't take too long for my name to get around and for the letters to start coming through the door offering trials. I did Scunthorpe, Brighton, Forest, Ipswich, Hull, Derby and Blackburn Rovers. Scunthorpe actually offered me terms. The conversation with the youth coach makes me laugh even now.

"Keegan started here, lad."

And that was about the extent of their pitch. They offered me £8 a week, which would go up to £10 after a year. I didn't consider it much of a loyalty bonus and, besides, Blackburn came in at the same time with a £16 rising to £18 offer. No contest. It wasn't just the money, though it played a part. Scunthorpe was much closer to home but Blackburn seemed a much better opportunity for me.

My dad was pretty astute in the negotiations. He always said I should never sign schoolboy forms with anyone because it might tie me up and that I should wait instead for apprentice terms. He was even cagey about Boston United. Howard Wilkinson was manager there when I was in my last year at school and because my dad knew the club secretary he wangled it for me to train with the club. Howard asked me to sign on as a non-contract player but I didn't want any problems if a league club came in for me.

"No, no, there'll be no problems like that."

He was true to his word. I did sign the forms but four weeks later I was a Blackburn Rovers apprentice. No money changed hands, not a penny. I know the families of youngsters now can be offered six-figure sums as sweeteners towards them pledging their sons' futures. Maybe there was some of that knocking about then, but I'm not so sure. I was about to turn sixteen and everything I'd ever dreamed of was now in my hands. My family wasn't well-off but we were never skint, and mum and dad worked hard to make sure it stayed that way. They, like me, were just delighted I'd been given the chance. Looking back it was probably naïve, but for me and my parents money always lagged way behind happiness in the important-things-in-life stakes. My view then, as it was throughout my career, was that I had the chance to play football for a living. Cash was always a side-issue. Well, nearly always.

I genuinely don't regret that at all. People used to ask me why I didn't go for a transfer and pick up a signing-on fee. But it was simple - I was on a good wage and I was playing football. I never used to look beyond the next season, never even considered retirement. I thought it would never end. I was perfectly happy just to go out and kick a ball.

2

MOVING
1976 to 1979

I WAS SIXTEEN-YEARS-OLD and leaving home. It was a wrench because I didn't know anyone in Blackburn but I did know I was joining a professional football outfit with a fantastic history. It might not have been Liverpool or Manchester United, but it wasn't Scunthorpe either.

I coped well. My dad had always been on the road a lot and I'd become used to being away from home because of all the trials I was doing, which usually meant two weeks away at a time, but I still missed mum and Nanny Garner. We were a close family in the sense that we got on well and shared interests, but we were also strong enough for me, like my brother, to move away and for that sense of belonging to remain. And, let's be honest, this was what I'd always wanted and to play football I'd have to move out earlier than most of my friends; break the family bonds sooner. And that was fine - I was a footballer now.

It's daft really. There's a saying: you can't always do what you like, but try to like what you do. I was planning a future where I could have my cake and eat it, where I could wake up in the morning and think 'bloody hell, I'm playing football today - and they're paying me to do it!' That was a good feeling.

The apprentices lived in a terraced house on Nuttall Street, right next to Ewood Park. There was a Hovis television advert some years ago with a shot of a football ground and cobbled streets. That was the Blackburn End entrance of Ewood Park on Nuttall Street. When Jack Walker redeveloped the ground the house was demolished. Given the current facilities for young Blackburn players, I doubt if it's missed much.

Four or five of us lived there. Connie would come in and cook breakfast for us, wash up and then come back and fix us an evening meal. Other than that we were left alone. Which is a dangerous thing to do with a bunch of kids under any circumstances, but with a bunch of kids who thought they were going to be the next George Best . . . There were a load of pensioners along the street though, and I'm sure the club used to pay them to keep an eye on us.

As an apprentice you had to get to work early. It's a funny word to use, and it didn't often feel like a job, but it did up at Altham. We'd be at the training pitch, which was five miles away behind Accrington Stanley's ground, for nine each morning. The routine was fairly monotonous, but we did get to train at the same place as the pros. I was learning and my appetite for improvement never dimmed throughout my career.

We'd get the kit ready at Ewood, load it on to the minibus, take it up to Altham, put it out ready for the senior players, clean everything up when they finished at lunch-time, put the gear back in the minibus, come back to Ewood and do all the jobs back at the ground. Boot cleaning, that sort of thing. If we were lucky we were finished for three in the afternoon.

The contrast from then to now is incredible. Blackburn have one of the finest Academy set-ups in the country, if not the world. There's a bunch of pitches, all identical in size to the one at Ewood, a swimming pool, an indoor pitch, fantastic catering facilities, accommodation for the youngsters, a gym, physio rooms ... everything. The new stadium is what the fans will point to as being the lasting legacy of Jack - that and the memories of the Championship - but for players, those kinds of training facilities mean everything.

It shows just how far one man's passion can take something. In my first autumn at Blackburn, when I'd only been there a couple of months, the club was briefly banned from entering the transfer market by the FA because of some payment irregularities. In under 20 years the same club broke the British transfer record twice to buy Alan Shearer and Chris Sutton.

If life as a footballer was sometimes dull, at least it wasn't like having to go to a factory every morning. We got enough early finishes and snooker was the preferred entertainment for the apprentices, mainly because it was cheap. A couple of scousers, Billy Riley and Chris Johnson, Mark Stein from Scotland, and Winston Small from Leeds were the lads I hung around with in those first few months. We had a good time but there's no question there's a lot of pressure on. It says something that only Mark and I were offered professional terms, and he only lasted a year. That's not unusual. Poor Winston was a great player and the club had big hopes for him. Then he broke his leg and that was the end of his career. Despite the fun and the excitement, it was a fragile existence which could be cruel.

In the early days I only knew other players. We were together so much of the time that I didn't have the opportunity to make friends from Blackburn. We'd try to get out in the evenings but we didn't have much money and, despite what people might think, we were pretty well behaved during the week. After Connie had made tea we'd nip out to the Fernhurst, a pub just a couple of minutes' walk from

Nuttall Street, for a game of pool and a lime and lemonade. The landlady was a real Bet Lynch type, a brassy scouser who kept the regulars in check and knew who we were. I think she might have been another spy because she'd maybe let us have the occasional lager, but that was about it.

Our serious drinking nights were Saturdays at the Cavendish nightclub in the shopping centre. People in Blackburn have long memories. It's been called Romeo and Juliet's, Utopia and all sorts of other things since those days, but it's still known as The Cav by kids who weren't even born when that name died.

My stay on Nuttall Street was pretty short. The next group of Charlie George wannabes were on their way and after about six months the club turfed us out and we were billeted with families.

Spinach. I still hate it to this day. Mr and Mrs Watson from Darwen were a lovely old couple, but so set in their ways. Mondays: steak and kidney pie. Tuesdays: liver and onions. Wednesdays: sausage and mash. Week in, week out. And spinach. Every bloody day. Well, maybe not every day, but enough to put me off for life. Spinach. Bloody spinach. I bloody hate the stuff. Mr Watson was much older than his wife and had a heart attack while I was there which left him bedridden and me looking for a new place to live.

Next stop was Trevor Close on the Wimberley Estate in Blackburn, a modern, well-looked-after council estate, with Harry and Hilda Wilkinson. They were a lot more family-orientated than the Watsons, who'd never had children. They had three kids, all a bit older than me, and they were great to live with - easy-going and big Blackburn Rovers fans.

Thinking back, it was hardly glamorous. But then, neither was the club at the time. We had to get to training on the bus once we'd left Nuttall Street and pay for it out of our own pockets. I was always skint but fortunately there was a tobacconist on the corner at Darwen Circus who sold fags in singles. God knows how else I'd have managed!

The youth team coach was John Pickering. Once we'd got all the kit together for the seniors we'd start our training, but pretty much on our own, separate from the first team who'd work with Jim Smith and Norman Bodell, his assistant. Jim was great and John was a superb youth coach, but Norman was just feeble.

"I think you've said it all Jim."

That was his standard response to just about anything Jim ever asked him. We never had much contact with Jim or Norman and, to be honest, I'm not even sure if they knew our names. They'd come and watch the odd youth team game on a Saturday morning and ask Pick for reports, but that was about as close as the youth players got. Norman fancied himself too. The trouble was that he couldn't keep it to himself - one of the lads found a picture of him modelling underwear in a Grattan catalogue and pinned it to the notice board.

I played every Saturday, mostly for the A team which was the apprentices' side, and sometimes there were a few pros coming back from injury who were selected. The games took place at Pleasington playing fields, just out of the town centre where the first team later did a lot of training. Fairly quickly I was getting the odd game in the reserves and I became a regular after about six months. That was where I really started to play as a striker having started out as a midfielder, a position I also played for a while when I got promoted to the first team.

I didn't have a problem with the switch from apprentice to reserve level, probably because my time at Boston had served me well. Although I'd only ever trained with them, I was used to playing with older, more experienced players since a very young age. A lot of pros who were released by the likes of Grimsby or Scunthorpe would find a home at Boston and I learnt a lot from them.

Howard Wilkinson was the player-manager at Boston and we'd train Tuesday and Thursday nights for an hour or so. It was running, running and running. It was a treat just to get the ball at your feet. He was renowned for running then and renowned for running when he went into the pro game. When Howard was manager at Leeds United they'd arrive in Blackburn on the night before the game, get down to Ewood for a session and then he'd make them run twelve laps round the pitch. Bloody running. Why not give 'em a ball? He was right to concentrate on fitness but wrong to leave it at just that.

The main football culture shock involved in moving to Blackburn was the mix of training styles and the fact we were at it most days. It was exhausting.

"To start with you'll get very tired because your body's getting used to training full-time."

I liked John Pickering. He was honest and he was right. Training virtually every day and playing at least once a week nearly killed me. I was knackered for a month, but there was a ball at my foot at least some of the time. I never much looked forward to Mondays and Tuesdays though, as they were the physical days, the hard days. The rest of the week was given over to ball work and tactics and this was where Pick really shone - he was one of the main influences on my game. After a mid-week reserve game, Jim spoke to me in the tunnel.

"Right, I'm going to take you to Southampton on Saturday for the last league game of the season. Nothing to play for. I'm going to give you your debut."

THERE'S ONLY ONE SIMON GARNER

It wasn't exactly out of the blue because I'd been playing well and I knew Jim had been saying a few nice things about me. All the same, I was chuffed to bits. Or I would have been.

"I can't play boss."

Jim and Pick, who'd been standing with me, looked at each other and then at me. An explanation was required. I think they thought I was taking the mickey and I wish that had been the case. In those days you either signed Football Association forms or Football League forms. If you signed FA forms, your club had to give you £250 as a kind of welcoming arrangement. If you signed League forms, it was £500. I was coming up to 17 and they had to offer me some kind of professional deal but, hardly the richest club in those days, I scrawled on the FA's dotted line and not the League's. No signature. No right to play in the League. No debut. And nobody had told Jim. The single benefit was that I got a pay rise to £45 a week. Blimey - I was nearly rich! I finally did sign the league forms that summer but it was more than a year before I got another chance with the first team, by which time Jim Smith had left and the club was in freefall to Division Three.

It was terrible. It was the spring of 1978, we were well-placed in the league and then Jim upped and offed to Birmingham. He said he was disappointed that the crowd didn't react well to a side that was playing well. There may have been more to it, but I was still young and not party to the gossip around the place. But let's not forget, Birmingham finished the season mid-table in Division One and Jim had arrived at Blackburn from his first league job at Colchester. For Blackburn it was a disaster but as a career move for Jim, you could understand it. Norman the yes-man took over for a period and then he waltzed off to Birmingham too.

MOVING

The big replacement? Jim Iley. From Barnsley. What a shambles. We finished the season fifth. I've not many nice things to say about Iley, but he was the man who gave me my belated debut.

It was a big shock. Obviously Jim Smith thought I was up to the job and there was a link through him back to Boston but managerial changes were something I, like most players, had to get used to. Jim looked after me too. I'd had a bit of trouble when I was an apprentice from Pick because of my smoking.

"You've got to stop smoking. I'm going to tell the manager."

I thought 'piss off John, I'm not at school'. I carried on smoking and he found out again.

"Go and see the manager."

So I had to go and see Jim. I went up into the Bald Eagle's nest which, like the apprentice accommodation, was in Nuttall Street.

"Come in Simon."

I sat down.

"What's this about you smoking?"

I blabbed something or other and watched him, sitting behind his desk, sucking on a fat cigar.

"Look Simon, Pick wants me to sack you. He's serious. But I'm not going to do that. Just be careful when you're smoking - don't get caught."

Then he offered me a cigar.

Iley wasn't built so leniently. He was a very dour, very down-to-earth Yorkshireman with absolutely no sense of humour. Compared to Iley, even Howard Wilkinson was like Ken Dodd. His training methods were frankly bizarre and, worse still, he didn't seem to know anyone's name.

THERE'S ONLY ONE SIMON GARNER

One of our big stars at the time was Stuart Metcalfe. He was local, which always helped, he'd been with the club forever and he was a fantastic footballer, one of the best midfielders I've ever been on a pitch with. Rumours regularly used to fly around about Metty being tracked by this, that or the other First Division club, particularly when he was a bit younger. He was one of the older pros who I really got on well with and he took me under his wing. A few of them did. And we had a shared interest in afternoon snooker sessions. And afternoon drinking sessions. And, best of all, afternoon drinking sessions in the snooker club.

"Number ten. NUMBER TEN. Get round there now and get it done."

That was how Iley addressed his players. By their tracksuit numbers. Metty was number ten. We'd been running round these two pitches at Brockhall Hospital in the days before Jack Walker developed some of the grounds into training facilities - there was a hill that Iley made us run up and down. It was more like doing an assault course than football training because we had to go round the pitches, up the hill, back down again, jump some hurdles, stop, do some press-ups, and start all over again. The more I think about it the more sane Wilkinson's methods seem.

"Send 'em round again."

Bonkers. Bloody bonkers. Perhaps the location got to him. He just about finished Metty off at Blackburn which was a disgrace. He dropped him to the bench. Another disgrace. Then he upset Dave Wagstaff who was an absolute hero in the '70s for Blackburn and he went off to Blackpool. The only bright spot, and it was a selfish one, was that while he didn't know me from Adam he gave me my debut.

MOVING

August 29, 1978. St James' Park, Exeter. League Cup. Exeter City 2 Blackburn Rovers 1. Garner plays in midfield and doesn't do an awful lot to catch the eye. Exeter's manager was Bobby Saxton, who later managed at Blackburn, and their side featured Vince O'Keefe in goal, who became and remains a very good friend after he signed for Blackburn, and Colin Randell, who also moved north to Ewood Park.

September 9, 1978. St James' Park, Newcastle. League Division Two. Newcastle United 3 Blackburn Rovers 1. Garner comes on as a substitute for John Aston and sees his first four minutes of league action.

September 16, 1978. Ewood Park, Blackburn. Blackburn Rovers 1 Leicester City 1. Full league debut about which I remember nothing whatsoever.

Just how barmy was Jim Iley? I was playing at Cardiff City some time that autumn. It was 0-0 and there were about five minutes to go before half-time. A long ball came over the top. I was chasing it down. It bounced just outside the area and the goalie came charging out. I'm going for it and I'm thinking 'he's going to nail me'. I just stopped. He clattered me anyway, but self-preservation kept me from breaking any bones. We got a free-kick and scored from it. Iley wouldn't let up in the dressing room at the break.

"You chickened out, you soft bastard."

There wasn't much I could say, I was a kid. But I'd had a good half and I'd won a free-kick in a good position. If I'd kept running I'd have almost certainly picked up a serious injury. More to the point, I didn't chicken out. Aggression has its place in football, but you have to know where the line is. It was as though he didn't know the first thing about the game. It didn't take long to realise he wasn't too hot on the second, third and fourth things either.

THERE'S ONLY ONE SIMON GARNER

But I was still on a high. I was in the side. Blackburn Rovers, though, were on a big downer and we were heading out of the division.

November 1, 1978. Jim Iley is sacked. Big sighs of relief from everyone. The campaign in the Lancashire Evening Telegraph by Dave Allin, who was writing about Blackburn Rovers at the time, had been vitriolic to say the least. It was clear Iley was disliked by the media and the fans and he was far from popular with the players. Despite the breaks I got under him, I was as happy as anyone to see the back of him.

November 3, 1978. Craven Cottage, south-west London. A Friday night. Fulham needed to win to go top. We were bottom and without a manager. Fulham 1 Blackburn Rovers 2. Garner scores twice for Blackburn Rovers, his first goals at senior level. The opener was a doddle. For some reason, the keeper went flying out of his goal onto the wing. Kevin Hird, who we later sold for £375,000 to Leeds - an enormous sum at the time - went past him and squared the ball. I tapped into an empty net at the open end of the ground from twelve yards. For the second, the ball was clipped over the top and I smacked it in from twenty yards. A fine goal! Even Pick, who picked the team that night, said so.

It was a strange period for me. I'd broken into the team but it felt as if a revolving door had been put into the manager's office. Pick was eventually given the job on a full-time basis and, despite the problems over my taste for nicotine, he knew me well enough as a player and as a person because of our time together in the youth team. More to the point, he liked what he saw on the pitch. I don't think we ever really hit it off, but there was a mutual respect - except that I could never see him being a manager. A coach certainly, but not a manager. He called me into his office for something or other soon after getting the job.

MOVING

"Hiya Pick, what's up?"

"No, Simon. You call me boss from now on."

The point he was making was a fair one, but it was like he was talking to a stranger. Sadly, that set the tone for his brief career as manager of the club. The trouble is, it takes something really special to be a football manager, something players really respect. And Pick didn't have it. Brilliant coach, crap manager. Perhaps that was Ray Harford's problem at Blackburn as well. He was an outstanding coach, everything ticked under him when he and Kenny Dalglish were at the club, but once Kenny stepped aside it quickly went to pieces.

John just didn't have the strength of character to release players. To end a youngster's career must be heartbreaking, but it has to be done. And it has to be done by the manager, not the youth team coach. So Pick had gone to a position where he was sacking the kids he'd been nurturing. It really didn't work out for him. And despite the fact he wasn't making a particularly good fist of managing the club it was difficult not to have a lot of sympathy for him.

It was a good season for me though. I played twenty or so games and scored eight goals, which wasn't a bad return for my first season in the first team. I felt as though I'd proved myself, which at that age was more important to me than the fact we were struggling badly. The flip-side to that was the way the name on the manager's office door kept on changing. And so I kept having to prove myself again. I was young though, and I suppose the arrogance of youth kept me going. I never doubted my own abilities and felt that whoever came next would like me as much as the previous boss. As you get older that changes. If you're in your thirties and a new man arrives you start to wonder where you're going to fit into the picture. I know because it eventually did for my professional career when I genuinely thought I could have been useful for another season or so at Wycombe Wanderers. Alan Smith felt differently.

Blackburn were relegated. It should have made me miserable, but it didn't. I'd achieved the first stage of my ambitions by being selected regularly at Blackburn. I'd also had the chance to play with some of my heroes. Like most clubs, we had a mixture of youth and experience on the books. But some of those older players were legends. John Radford was one, he'd won the Double with Arsenal. Duncan McKenzie was another, he was one of the most gifted players of his generation. Unfortunately it was an era when skill and grace were not the most sought after attributes for international selection.

Pick once took us to Ireland for a break. I was the youngest there and I was rooming with Raddy. He liked a drink and so we stayed up most of the night boozing with John Bailey. When we got back to Blackburn we had a big meeting down at the training ground. Pick wasn't best pleased, he'd obviously heard about the session which, to be honest, was no big deal.

"Garner, I'm fining you two weeks wages. I'm not standing for that kind of behaviour."

And then Raddy had his two penn'orth. It was like a scene from Spartacus

"He had a drink but so did I. If you're going to fine him two weeks wages, you fine me two weeks wages. It was my idea to stay up."

And I'm thinking 'go on Raddy, get him told'. It was like my dad sorting out a school bully. Maybe that's one of the reasons Pick fell out with him. Raddy was a strong character. He said what he wanted to say. He was the union rep as well and I think he felt he owed it to the other players to stand up for them. He certainly wouldn't let me be pushed around because I was a kid. Where Pick went wrong though, was in not fining either of us. It was, strictly speaking, an offence. He should have stood his ground and carried out the threat. He didn't. He was never going to make a manager.

McKenzie was a great fella. And he liked a cigarette too so we had something in common straight away. He cost us £80,000, a club record which stood for years. Everyone knew he was a fine player, but he was still best known for the fact he'd jumped over a Mini. For me though, the fact he smoked was brilliant and he was my lookout on the team bus. No one was going to tell him to put a fag out, but I'd have been dropped on from a large height if I'd have been caught. It was like being at school. It still is - Suzy, my wife, made me go outside for a cigarette before I finally stopped this year. And Duncan, like Raddy, was brilliant to play with. He really helped me along. I played him through for a goal at Wrexham and he spoke to a newspaper afterwards.

"He's the best striker I've seen outside the First Division."

That made me feel fantastic. Duncan was different from the rest of us, basically because he had money. There was no jealousy though and he was well-liked. He was just a bit more polished than the rest of us which, given he'd played for Leeds, Everton, Chelsea and abroad, was hardly surprising. As soon as you went into his house near Haydock Park you knew it wasn't like your own. There was all this fantastic furniture which he'd shipped in from abroad and a nice car in the drive. A drive - that was posh! For a while, when I was playing with the likes of these guys, it was easy to let the mind wander...

"There's Radford, storming through the middle, looking as fit as he ever did in his Arsenal days, he lays it off for Garner, who side-steps the United defence and - what a goal! Simon

Garner, his twenty-fifth of the season, a magnificent strike with his left foot. The keeper had no chance. It's Blackburn Rovers 3 Manchester United 0. Surely now Rovers have won the FA Cup."

Putting the dreams to one side, I had to concentrate on retaining my place. We'd had three managers in a 12-month period and with each switch there was a period of change and uncertainty. I think that's why I sought security off the field and, at a very young age, got married.

I met Mandy in The Beechwood, a pub on Livesey Branch Road, which is close to Ewood Park. They had a fantastic disco on Mondays which became a big night out for a lot of the younger players. We married soon after in November 1978, a month after I'd scored my first senior goal and just a couple of weeks after Jim Iley was sacked. Ron Greenwood, a somewhat more successful manager, once said he liked his players to be settled down - it was a fair point because I cut back on the boozing and got into the best shape of my life.

We got married at the registry office in Blackburn and had a reception at the Kiosk in Sunnyhurst Woods in Darwen. It says something about how football salaries have progressed because we couldn't afford a photographer so my brother David took the pictures - or thought he had. After spending what seemed like hours arranging all kinds of different family groupings we found out a couple of days later that he'd forgotten to put a film in the camera.

Looking back I sometimes wonder what I thought I was doing. I was nineteen and a professional footballer - what on earth made me get married? It was simple really. Nanny Garner was old and I desperately wanted to give her a grandchild and Mandy's family wanted to see a ring on her finger. I think Mary, Mandy's mum, was quite keen on the idea of her daughter marrying a footballer because it gave her some local celebrity status. It was one of her ambitions to see her daughter married to someone rich or famous. I didn't really fit into either category, but I was the closest thing in that part of town.

3

STAYING
1979 to 1981

WE WERE RELEGATED with four games still to play, which is dismal by anyone's standards, and Pick was ousted. Then Howard Kendall - one of the great names of football - was hired for his first job in management. It was a real coup to get him and it was a breath of fresh air having him at the club. He was still playing well and he'd been coaching at Stoke City, so a move to Blackburn as player-manager looked a good deal for everyone.

It was good to have a boss who still had a foot in the players' camp. He liked a drink and he was always with the boys. If we were socialising, he was socialising with us. And he loved to take us on trips. We'd always had them, but Howard would get us away two or three times a season. Mind you, it mostly seemed like little more than an excuse to arrange a big piss-up for his mates. There was one trip to Jersey and, strangely enough, we played a friendly against Stoke and all his drinking buddies were there. One night in my room me, John Butcher, Noel Brotherston and Mick Rathbone were supping the tax-free vino and getting smashed when there was this incredible crash in the corridor; it sounded like someone had fallen down the stairs. An annihilated Kendall lurched through the door, landed in the corner, opened his mouth and slagged off each one of us in turn. Or so I'm told. I slept through my dressing-down and he didn't even notice.

STAYING

If he was lenient and good-natured away from the game, he was inspirational on the pitch. He demanded effort and concentration and gradually made us into a team that just wouldn't concede goals. We were like Arsenal and the 1-0 final score was a speciality. It didn't begin brightly though, and we were way down at the bottom of the table for a few weeks before we stabilised, and then in January we went on this incredible run where we got twenty-nine points out of thirty when it was just two points for a win - we even had time to knock Coventry of the First Division out of the FA Cup. At the heart of it all was a superb defence which Howard had developed, despite having to off-load some of the best defensive talent in the country. One of the first things he had to do when he came to the club was negotiate the sale of John Bailey to Everton. That meant two of our best players, John and Kevin Hird, both attacking full-backs, had been stripped from the team in a few months. He was a canny operator though, and brought in Jim Branagan who was solid as a rock. We also had Mick Rathbone, Glenn Keeley and Derek Fazackerley at the back with Jim Arnold in goal. It was a backline which, by and large, stood us in good stead for years. In midfield it was the likes of Howard and Duncan McKenzie, and then there was me, Noel Brotherston and Andy Crawford in contention up front. It was a great team and way too hot for Division Three. We finally got promoted in a game at Bury when Crawford scored twice.

Crawford scored 18 goals that season, he was electric. But what a tosser. Howard bought him and Jim Branagan early in his first season. Jim came from Huddersfield and Crawford was nabbed out of Derby's reserve team. Jim replaced Kevin Hird which was a hell of a tough task. He didn't instantly bond with the fans, mainly because he wasn't Kevin, but also due to the fact that he wasn't all that quick, didn't have much of a first touch and treated the half-way line like it had been fenced off with electrified barbed wire. But he was a fantastic team man - reliable, honest, determined and passionate. He was underrated yet he did everything Howard asked of him and he eventually became a real fans' favourite; at the end of the day, if a player is committed he'll win over the supporters.

Crawford, on the other hand, was a jumped-up prima donna. Nobody knew him at all. He'd come in to training at ten o'clock, walk through the door, not speak to anybody, get changed next to the door, train, come back, have a shower and leave - all in virtual silence. There were stories going round that after every game he'd go back to his Nuttall Street terraced house and write a report of how well he'd done in the game. He wouldn't even have a drink with us - in a bloody Howard Kendall team! He wasn't a team man at all and as long as he scored in the game he wasn't bothered. I played up front with him and he wouldn't even talk on the pitch. I'd been used to playing with experienced pros like John Radford and Joe Craig, a former Scottish international who had partnered Kenny Dalglish up front at Celtic, and these were players who helped me out, showed me the tricks. Being in their shadows was fine, they'd proved themselves, but I wasn't happy about playing second fiddle to this egomaniac.

Raddy had gone by now though, and Joe struggled to get a game under Howard. He never really clicked at Ewood but I bled him for knowledge and ways of improving my own game. Still, Joe and I managed to squeeze in a last bit of teamwork. His wife was in the next room to Mandy at Queens Park Hospital when our babies were due in February 1981. I sat outside, smoking and scared, he was in with his wife throughout. It's the same on a football pitch. If one player's looking a bit out of sorts, then another has to make up for it. Or something! Well it wasn't my fault. I would love to have been there, I really would. Only I can't stand the sight of blood. So next door there's all this screaming coming from Joe's wife and I've got Mandy twitching about with only a trainee nurse for company. I wanted to be in the pub. Or anywhere but where the action was.

"Right Mr Garner, put one leg up on your shoulder, I'll have the other leg."

"No, sorry love. I can't stomach blood. I'm not stopping here. You'll have to get someone else to hold that leg. I'm feeling a bit faint."

That's when I left Mandy to give birth to John. While she did all the work, I rolled down the corridor, bounced off the walls, found the waiting-room, collapsed in a corner, smoked twenty John Player Specials and became a dad. Strangely, blood and injuries never bothered me in a game. Too much adrenaline to notice maybe, or too focused on the game. But real blood in real life is a wholly different matter. Even the thought of real blood in real life is enough to make my stomach turn. I was at the snooker club one afternoon when some bloke was talking about an operation he was going to have on his eye, about having a needle pushed into it. The next thing I remember is being woken up in the toilet. I hadn't had a single drink, I just passed out thinking about the operation. All of which, perhaps, contributes to my swift exit from the delivery suite. It was the same when Mandy had James, though I did manage to stay upright - and in the delivery suite - when Suzy, the present Mrs Garner, had Thomas in August 2001.

I was only young, just twenty-one, but I really took to being a dad. I'd wanted to be a dad for so long and it didn't disappoint me. Football's a good job for fatherhood because you don't start work until ten in the morning and get most afternoons off, so I probably saw more of my boys as babies than most fathers could dream of. I'd play with John in the mornings before training and take him on long walks in the afternoons, usually just the two of us. I never really had anywhere special to amble to, it was just the doing it that mattered. And I didn't really miss the snooker sessions or whatever other diversion the players had planned. I'd sometimes show my face at the snooker club, but not every day like it used to be. As a family we were strong and we lived in a new house just opposite the Shadsworth council estate. Mandy wasn't working so we saw a lot of each other, and her parents visited a lot and helped us out. It was a very settled period of my life outside the game. I missed my own folks, but it was virtually impossible for me to visit them because they were both working, so I spoke to them every night without fail.

Strikers seemed to come and go at Ewood Park and most of them made very little impression, but there were some stalwarts in other positions who, like me, became part of the fixtures and fittings. Mick Rathbone, who is John's godfather, was one of them. There was no reason why we should get on, but we did. While I roomed with Mick for six or seven years, his absolute devotion to ultimate fitness never rubbed off on me at all. On away trips he'd get up early and go for a jog or do some stretching while I'd be having a lie-in looking forward to a bacon butty. For Mick, a lot of it was nervous energy. On Sundays he'd get up at the crack of dawn, get down to the railway station and pick up the first edition of the Sunday People. If they'd given him a mark under six he'd be in a state of depression until the next game. His dark periods weren't as bad as John Butcher's though. John wasn't a bad keeper, but he had no consistency. And he was trying to fill Paul Bradshaw's boots after Paul had to be sold because the club was in a financial hole. Some people blamed John for us not going up in 1978, but that's way too harsh and some of the stick he got from the fans was awful. It can be soul-destroying for a player and the feeling runs through the team because while everyone wants to help, nobody wants to appear to be a patronising git.

Howard knew how to help though, in all sorts of ways. He understood players and what they needed. I think we could have had any set of players that season and Howard would have taken us up. He injected a new life into Blackburn Rovers. He even got me to enjoy training. For a start there was no more of this bloody running round in circles.

"Right. That's it. I'm knackered."

Howard had run about 400 yards and was breathless. It was the longest training run we did all season. Instead of having us yomp up and down hills, he put the ball at our feet and drilled into us the defensive approach to winning football. It left the strikers with few chances, and we had to do our share of defending - or some of us did because Crawford didn't want to get involved in all that rough tackling nonsense, he just wanted to stand up front and score goals. So he did, the bastard. Oh, and Duncan never really liked that sort of negative attitude either. But that was different - I liked Duncan and he was getting on a bit! And, of course, there's the small fact of what Duncan could offer us in terms of tricks and turns, his flair and the killer pass he could pluck from nowhere. If promotion back to Division Two was never a formality, it wasn't far off, and I wish I could remember the party we had after finally clinching it. I can't even remember where the trip was, except that we bought the cerveza with pesetas and drank ourselves stupid for a whole week. Except Crawford, who always found a reason to stay at the hotel.

THERE'S ONLY ONE SIMON GARNER

It wasn't the biggest surprise that he asked for a transfer during pre-season, despite the fact the fans loved him. Scoring eighteen goals in a debut season, one every other game, is going to make you a hero. But he thought he was better than Blackburn Rovers and his dad made no secret of it either. He didn't even turn up for pre-season training, he just went off somewhere to train by himself. He eventually moved on to join those giants of the south, Bournemouth, and scraped a living at places like Stockport, Torquay and Poole. Bless him.

I thought I was following him out of Ewood Park too, but not out of choice. Howard was trying to impose himself more on the side in his second season. And it worked. In the first nine games of the season we won seven and drew two which would have been an achievement for any club, but we'd only just been promoted. I wasn't a regular, but I was knocking on the door. Or so I thought. Part of the rebuilding involved Duncan leaving and a permanently sun-tanned Viv Busby coming in. And, it seemed, me going to Halifax.

"You'll never play for this club again."

Howard had a way with words. He wanted to sign somebody from Chesterfield, a big centre forward. They wanted something like £40,000 for him, but Howard didn't have that kind of money available. Maybe £10,000, maybe £20,000, but nothing like £40,000. Howard then got a bid of £30,000 from Halifax for me - problem solved for Howard. If he can get me out. He told me about the offer on the phone.

"No thanks, boss."

I simply didn't want to leave Blackburn. I was settled with a home, a wife and a new baby. More to the point, Halifax was the sort of team that was always near the bottom of the league with the threat of being booted out hanging over them. I went over for a look though, because Howard hadn't given me much option - according to him, I was never going to play for Blackburn again. The pitch was magnificent, one of the best I'd ever seen, but the stadium was teetering on collapse. George Kirby was the manager. I went into his so-called office, which was about the size of a kitchen table, and squeezed into a chair to hear his pitch.

"I want you to sign, Simon, I want you in the side for Saturday."

"I'll think about it."

"Well think quickly, Simon. I need you to sign by two o'clock then you can go straight into the team."

It was noon.

"No. I need to speak to my wife about this."

"Well call her then."

"She's out shopping."

She wasn't, but it seemed gentler than telling him the truth - that I thought Halifax were crap and there was as much chance of me signing for George as there was of me signing for Burnley.

"Well call the police to go and find her."

He was desperate.

"Look, if you want to sign me you can wait for another game. I want to think about this."

I went back to Blackburn and straight to the manager's room.

"How did you go on?"

"I'm not happy about it. I'm not going."

Howard was desperate too; he really wanted this bloody giant from Chesterfield.

"How much do you want from the transfer fee?"

Oh, bloody hell.

"Halifax have offered me a good deal, boss."

They had. It was a £10,000 signing-on fee which was an enormous sum.

"You'll have to give me another £10,000 as well. Then I'll think about it."

"I don't know, Simon. Get out."

I was at home when the phone went. Howard was offering me £5,000 to go. Add that to the £10,000 from Halifax and the company car and the free use of an apartment, and it was adding up to an attractive offer, but Howard was missing the point. The money really wasn't the issue and I'd only given him the £10,000 figure because I knew there was no way that he could have managed it. Short term, of course, it was a very good deal. Long term, I'd be a non-league player driving a Reliant Robin within a couple of seasons.

"I mean it, Simon. You'll never play for Blackburn Rovers again."

And you're not going to be here forever, I thought. So I'll bide my time. Which, as is the way in football, I didn't have to do for long because Noel Brotherston, our left-footed genius and Northern Ireland international, broke his leg just after deadline day and the squad was already stretched. Howard had no choice but to pick me. While as a player you'd never wish injury on a colleague, you have to take whatever opportunities are put your way - and I did. It gave me another chance, and I even played wide on the left at first in Noel's position. There's no doubt that losing Noel cost us promotion. We'd looked like making it into the top flight, but Noel was central to what we did.

If Noel was the specific reason for us missing out, the more general cause was the fact we had virtually no money and a tiny squad. Tony Parkes was another broken-leg-casualty that season and while he was never a match-winner in the

Brotherston mould, he was supremely reliable and a fine ball-winner. But Noel missed the last nine matches of the campaign and we drew five of them 0-0. We missed promotion on goal difference.

It was sickening. We were within touching distance of playing Liverpool, Arsenal and Manchester United. Whatever problems I'd had with Howard were nothing compared to the feeling of losing this chance. I was distraught. We all were. And then it went from bad to worse. The rumours about Howard had started earlier in the season. There was a lot of talk about him taking the Crystal Palace job and I think they even came in with a formal offer, but there was no way he could turn down Everton. Within a week of the season finishing, he was gone. A superb manager, despite his poor taste in strikers, and our best player. Although I'm a natural optimist, I thought we might never recover from a loss like that.

4

COMPETING
1981 to 1985

NOBODY, AND I MEAN NOBODY, had heard of Bobby Saxton. Howard was one of the most famous names in the game and then in steps a complete unknown. For most of the players there was the worry that things were about to slow down again at the club after Howard's achievements. With him at the helm and Mick Heaton, who also left for Goodison Park, as his coach, we'd been an excellent side and one which was knocking on the golden gates of the First Division. Bobby's appointment could only be viewed as a backward step. But it wasn't a unanimous opinion because from a purely selfish point of view, and despite the obvious progress we'd made, I was relieved. There was no doubt in my mind that I would have been shipped out at the first opportunity by Howard. A new manager meant a clean slate for me.

So in comes Bobby and half of bloody Devon. Or that's how it felt when he filled up the backroom positions with his mates from Plymouth. There was Jim Bodell as his assistant, Howard Jarman, the new chief scout, and Tony Long as physio. And officially promoted to the coaching staff was Tony Parkes. The injury he sustained at, I think, Notts County was dreadful and ended his career. He was getting on a bit as a player, but that was a cruel end. But Tony was smart and he'd had his eye on a coaching role for a while and, like Derek Fazackerley, you always felt he'd do well at it.

COMPETING

But what a job for Bobby to come into. With Howard's profile it was always going to be a tough act to follow. It didn't help his cause that he really didn't like talking to the media. He wasn't being ignorant, it just wasn't in his nature to be the centre of attention except in the company of his players. Jim Iley. That's what I thought. Another bloody Jim Iley. Especially after he got us running in training again. Howard hated running, so we did hardly any. But Bobby was an intelligent coach and understood the sensitivities of the players, so the work was varied from the start. And he was also dedicated. He worked hard on tactics, explained himself well and always set up good shooting workouts for the strikers to go through at the end of a session. He wasn't a bad judge of players either, and he soon got to work building a team which pretty much stuck together during his time at Ewood.

Ian Miller was one of his earlier signings and cost £60,000, which was serious money considering how little Howard was prepared to let me go for. He was the first of many from the south-west and Bobby's connections in that area were clearly very solid, as were his reports on Dusty, or Windy as the fans called him. Lightning quick and a very direct wing player, he improved the team straight away. He might have been predictable because he hardly ever tried to beat a player on the inside as his left foot was useless, but for a striker predictability is an asset - knowing what he's going to do next puts you one step ahead of a defence which might not have done its homework.

I'd like to think a player like Ian could have seen us promoted the previous season because while we were very solid at the back, we too rarely broke free as an attacking force. He was also a grafter and worked well coming back, and he and Jim Branagan were an excellent combination on the right.

But while Bobby was calling on his old pals in the south-west, Howard was up to the same on Merseyside. He poached Jim Arnold, our keeper, which gave John Butcher another chance before Bobby stepped in for Terry Gennoe from Southampton. He was another player with no real history, but he became a superb long-term buy. Terry was incredibly dedicated. It was unheard of to have a keeper who would gladly stay behind to do extra training to help the strikers out, but there was an instant rapport and respect and it was a two-way street because it was no chore for me if Terry wanted to do some additional goalkeeping work. It paid off too. Terry's enthusiasm rubbed off on his back four who trusted him enormously, giving him the opportunity to command the box without having to resort to the kind of screaming and bawling of the likes of Peter Schmeichel.

Obviously with Bobby doing some spending, it wasn't long before the attacking line would welcome a new player and Norman Bell, who'd been known as the Wolves super-sub, was signed. He was great for me. A big, strong bloke who took a lot of pressure off and gave me the room to get the goals. He didn't score many himself though, and the fans were on his back which was unfair. I don't think they realised how hard he worked and how much effort he put into creating space for others to exploit by dragging defenders out of position. It had been a long time since I'd played with a big centre forward and I liked it - he helped me to fourteen goals that season.

Other signings Bobby made included Mickey Speight, a player in the Kendall mould, and Kevin Arnott, who came on loan from Sunderland. Kevin was an exceptional talent and had real vision. The only problem was that we just couldn't afford to buy him. What Bobby was looking for was a replacement for Howard, someone who could influence a game from the middle of the park. Because Howard was a genuinely class act, even though he was getting on, it meant we could build a team of grafters and battlers around him. Without him we didn't have anyone to really unpick an opposition when it really mattered, though Kevin, for the all-too-brief period he was with us, managed it. We had a dream start to the season and a pretty solid middle period as well. After the initial shock of getting another unknown manager, it took virtually no time to realise how good he really was, regardless of what the media thought. As an attacking force we were creating plenty of chances and that was largely down to Dusty, who would present us with four or five solid opportunities a game which was unheard of with Howard, whose strategy was less direct. But because we had pretty much the same defence, we were still strong at the back.

And then the wheels came off. We were in a promotion position well into the spring but we fell to pieces when Kevin went back to Sunderland. It wasn't all down to him going, but losing him and a couple of games soon after rattled our confidence. We finished the season tenth, which was hardly a disaster, but we knew we'd let ourselves down after the start we'd had. The atmosphere around the place never dipped though. Bobby just had this aura about him that inspired players and created a fantastic team spirit. There's nothing better than feeling you're an important cog in a well-oiled machine and that spreads a positive attitude throughout the team. Under Bobby we worked hard as a team and played hard as a team. There were no factions or unsettling influences and we stuck together through what had the potential to be a very tricky time.

That's not to say we didn't have our share of lads prepared to speak their mind and upset people here and there - but that was about trying to make things better. It was a professional and not a personal issue. Glenn Keeley definitely fell into this category. Hard as nails on the pitch, hard as nails off it. If he argued white was black, I'd agree with him. Then and now.

If Bobby's first season at Blackburn was a partial success, 1982-83 was almost utterly forgettable as a team event. The best things I can say are that I scored twenty-two league goals, my best season ever, I joined Alan Price on stage to sing Simon Smith And His Amazing Dancing Bear, and a bunch of nutcases from Burnley tried to dismantle part of Ewood Park.

Despite the goals the season pretty much passed me by. We picked up a couple of players cheaply - Colin Randell, a midfielder from Plymouth who was never going to set the world alight, and Vince O'Keefe as goalkeeping back-up to Terry.

Those signings told their own story and there was never much chance of us doing anything more than consolidating. In fact, it was the only season of my career when I felt we were only ever capable of achieving a mediocre mid-table position. There was no excitement of any kind because we were never in danger of either pushing for promotion, except for a brief early flurry, or trying to avoid relegation. We finished eleventh, we were utterly inconsistent and we were boring the pants off the few supporters who could be bothered to turn up. We never played to more than about 8,000 all season.

From a personal perspective, it could have been much worse because at least the fans liked me. Others weren't so lucky. A lot of the players didn't used to like playing next to the old Riverside Stand because they could pick out voices slagging them off all the time. Jim Branagan would get absolutely slaughtered sometimes and the crowd was so small you'd hear Jim screaming about the whingers during the game.

"It was him. That bastard in the hat. I'll bloody have him if he doesn't shut it."

I know we're all professionals and supposed to be able to take some stick, but it really affected the performance of some players like Norman Bell and, later on, Jimmy Quinn. But for the others, they just got on with the job and tried not to laugh because it was the same old voices with the same old whinges week after bloody week. The club was hardly well off in those days, which is one of the reasons I admire Bobby so much, and he somehow managed to keep spirits high.

Colin and Vince were hardly going to sell more season tickets so Bobby was under a lot of pressure to get success on the pitch to attract the crowds. Bill Fox, the chairman, had said in the summer that money for transfers would be based only on the number of people coming through the turnstiles. But you can hardly blame the fans for not falling for the bribe, they're not daft and we weren't giving them much to cheer. We were solid but dull to the point of tedium.

As well as being popular on the terraces, I could take some comfort from the fact that I was improving as a player under Bobby. He made me realise I didn't have to run round the pitch like a headless chicken all afternoon. He slowed me down and made me much more aware of positioning and timing.

"Just save your energy a bit, Simon, and get in the box more."

Which was pretty easy. Noel Brotherston and Ian Miller were dreadfully inconsistent but both, on their day, were fantastic. Noel was incredible and had the ability to turn good players inside out and make them look stupid. He wasn't quick, like Dusty who'd knock the ball past his marker and start running, but he really knew how to get round players. And he stuck at it. If it wasn't his day, he'd just keep on trying, always looking for the killer pass. Dusty, though, could let his head drop for the rest of the game if his first cross wasn't half decent.

In truth, none of us got going that season and after Christmas we went to pieces again. Even Kevin Arnott, who came for a second loan spell, couldn't make the difference this time. And it didn't help that this was the era of the plastic pitch, a surface on which we never won a single game. The pitch at QPR was crap. It was bone-hard and it was like playing on concrete. We performed like we had our feet in the stuff.

Still, Bobby liked to keep us entertained. On trips he made sure we got the best hotels and did everything he could to make sure we enjoyed ourselves. We'd compete most years in the Lancashire Manx Cup on the Isle of Man and we'd always stay at the Palace Hotel, I think it was called, where there was a casino and a cabaret. Alan Price was performing and the audience had been a bit rowdy, which we didn't help by standing at the back of the hall singing along.

"This is my show and if you want to sing, that's fine, but I'll go home and leave you to it."

I really thought he meant it. But we were young and we were drunk, so when he started the next tune we joined in again and, true to his word, he stopped the performance. There were some hard looks directed at us from the rest of the audience but then he broke into a smile and insisted that if we thought we could hack it, we should join him on stage. I don't for a minute think he expected us to do it but, one by one, we trooped to the front of the auditorium, climbed the steps, and acted as his backing singers for the next song.

We didn't exactly bring the house down, but Burnley fans did their best towards the end of the season at Ewood Park. I doubt if I need to say this, but the atmosphere in those East Lancashire fixtures was nothing short of poisonous. People talk about Merseyside and Manchester, but I can't imagine a derby in England that has so much local honour at stake. Blackburn and Burnley are only ten miles apart but the people are proud of their own identities. The accents are different, the attitudes are different and there's no question of any divided loyalties - it's one team per town. There's no choice to be made about who you support like there is in Liverpool, Manchester or London. Here you're born with it.

So you can imagine the response of the Burnley fans when I missed a penalty and was then invited to retake it. I know every single one of those Burnley fans hated me at that moment and, to be honest, it was a pretty good feeling. But at the same time I know it was only a minority who tried to prevent the re-take. They climbed into the eaves of the Darwen End roof and started flinging slates on to the pitch. I've known some pretty stupid and pretty hairy things go on at games, but nothing compared to this - most of the missiles were raining down on their fellow supporters at the front. It was disgraceful. The players were taken off the field by the referee and Frank Casper, the Burnley manager, appealed for calm. Eventually matters settled and I stepped up for a second bite of the cherry. I scored. That was a sweet moment. We won the game 2-1 and Burnley were relegated a month later. Within four years they were just one game from going out of the league altogether, and, possibly, out of business too when they were rock bottom of the Fourth Division.

Towards the end of the season rumours about me and the club started to spread. Neither of them were helpful, and neither were true. Regarding me, a freelance journalist who I'd prefer not to name, came up with a story about me hitting the bottle and smashing up my house. It was based on the fact there was a pile of empty bottles outside my home and the windows had been removed. I've always had a good relationship with the media - national and local - and have always been happy to give an opinion or take part in an interview. I'd go so far as to say I enjoy it. But this story made me wary and I never again dealt with this operator. All he had to do was check a few facts. In fact he knew me well and simply had to ask, but he just wrote the story up and fired it across the sports pages of the national press. Mandy and I had thrown a party - that was why there were so many bottles. And we were having double-glazing installed - which accounts for the windows being out. For the sake of a few quid, we were subjected to some appalling stories.

The other rumour was that the club didn't want to get promotion because it didn't have the finance to support a season in Division One. This story popped up a few times over the years and I have to say I think it was absolute rubbish. Yes the club was poor, but under the likes of Bill Fox, who had recently become chairman, we had very ambitious men who wanted nothing but the best for the club. In fact, without people like Bill, who I considered a friend, we might have joined the Lancashire freefall. Blackpool, Preston, Burnley and Bolton were once, like Blackburn, among the soccer superpowers. The prudence and vision of the board at Blackburn ensured - against all the odds - that we never followed them to the brink of ruin and extinction. They all fell to the bottom divisions and have only recently stabilised. We never lacked the desire to be promoted, we simply weren't up to the job.

Chris Thompson joined us in the summer of 1983 from Bolton. He was another of those players people didn't know much about and he was never really that popular with the fans, but I liked him. He worked hard during the game without scoring many, but opened plenty of doors for me with the running he did off the ball. He was pretty much thrown straight in to the fray as well, which I think made his performances even more impressive.

His chance came after Norman Bell was injured in the first game of the season, a 2-2 draw with Huddersfield. Norman's knee was mangled and though he played some local non-league football after that his pro career was over. Another loss. He was never a big socialiser, but he was a great professional to work with and an honest, down-to-earth player who never shirked on the training field or in a game. Even when we played together a few times for the veterans, he still hated being substituted. So that was another striker I'd seen off, but not in the way I would have liked.

I learnt from these guys, Thommo included, and we formed a good partnership, despite the fact we had similar styles. In fact, with the single exception of Andy Crawford, all my partners helped me in my game in some way or other. It wasn't always an obvious thing, but as I got older and more established I got to understand the game better and how other strikers worked. I nicked their best tricks and later on they nicked mine.

No doubt about it, apart from our sloppy finale, this was a good season for Blackburn Rovers and served as a justification of Bobby's appointment. I was an ever present, which I only managed twice in my career, and I scored nineteen goals which is just short of one every other game - a pretty solid indicator of my form under Bobby. Mind you, five of the goals came in a single afternoon.

Saturday September 10, 1983, at home to Derby County. Final score: Blackburn Rovers 5 Derby County 1.

THERE'S ONLY ONE SIMON GARNER

My first came from a long ball over the top. Paul Futcher let it roll for the goalkeeper but he just stood there, rooted to the spot, and it was easy enough to take it round him and tap in. The second was a right foot shot and the fifth a penalty. It was a relief to see it go in because I'd missed a few, but I just whacked it and in it went. The other two? No idea, I just can't remember them at all. So what - the record books tell me I got all five and I'll settle for that! I'll never forget that afternoon and neither will Paul Futcher. Every time I played against him after that he seemed to set out with the intention of kicking me. Derby were a good side too. Archie Gemmill and John Robertson were still top-class players and Peter Taylor was a great manager.

Naturally enough I expected to be grabbing a few headlines in the Sunday papers so I went and bought them all. The only problem was that Tony Caldwell got five for Bolton as well so it all got a bit diluted. Still, I got the one and only freebie of my career that night when the boss at the Bull's Head, a pub and restaurant at the Whalley end of Blackburn, picked up my tab for dinner. Nice one.

I can't deny that it was in my head around that time that a move to Division One must have been on the cards. I was on great form and very sharp. I was never the fastest player but I could shield the ball well and make space - not unlike Kenny Dalglish, I used to persuade myself. And I was two-footed, which made me a little bit special. Five against a good side like Derby who were close to the top of Division Two and playing consistently well. I must have been in the frame. There were a few stories in the papers saying I was being watched by some of the big clubs but they were holding off for another season to see if I was the real deal. I've no idea if there was any truth in what they were saying and it was before the days when agents would tout players around, but I do know the club had always said it would be open with me and let me know if there was a top flight club in for me. And if I'm being honest, if someone had bid, say, half a million for me, then the club would have found it difficult to turn that kind of money down. Like any footballer I had the ambition to play against the best week-in, week-out but I always thought that eventually I'd do it with Blackburn. I just never imagined that when we did make it to the Premiership, I'd be leaving before the first ball had been kicked.

So back with my feet on the floor the club struggled along on the meagre resources it had available. Fortunately we were getting some good young players through the ranks and that was the only reason we managed to sustain a decent challenge in 1983/84. Simon Barker was a superb prospect from the first time I saw him play. He'd been doing well in the reserves and though he certainly wasn't the finished article, Bobby threw him into the first team. From his debut onwards he never looked out of place or out of his depth and he had a bag of tricks as big as the one he carried his confidence in. While Simon was never a big-head he had that assured presence which marked him out as a special player. He scored great goals from midfield, he was quick to help out in defence, he passed the ball superbly and he could run all day. In many respects he was the player who gave us back what we'd been missing since Howard left, a gap we could only fill temporarily with the likes of Kevin Arnott. It was obvious he'd play at the highest level and eventually had a great career with Queen's Park Rangers. He wasn't much of a tackler though, and he'd get stick from the crowd if he shirked a big challenge, but he was still a young lad and later in his career he added that element to his game. Mark Patterson started to emerge at about the same time. He lacked the speed of Dusty and the skills of Noel but he could get a cross in from anywhere. The coaching he got from Bobby helped him exploit a more limited game to the best effect. Mark never had the ability of Simon Barker - very few players did - but he had a powerful aggression which, most of the time, he kept just in check. It was the same in training where he was never too worried about letting off a few ripe challenges and I wasn't alone in learning to keep out of his way. He was a typical hard-working player who was never going to set the world on fire but would always get a move if he needed one. Which is why he played for such a lot of clubs and, with Sheffield United, even made it to the Premiership.

The season turned out to be another false dawn though, and we were undone by our usual dismal patch, this time coming towards the end of the season, which made it even more disappointing. We'd had a sixteen-match unbeaten run and we were bursting with confidence. The chances were falling well and we were scoring goals but we just gummed up from April, dropped out of contention and finished sixth. Too many draws. Just like under Kendall.

If it was a disappointing end to the season professionally, at home John got a baby brother, James, and life was rosy. We moved to Cherry Tree, a nice end of town and near to Pleasington. Now I had two lads to take out on my rambles.

There's just no way you can afford to relax as a player, as I'd been constantly reminded throughout my career, and despite having had another excellent season on a personal level my position was back under threat with the signing of another striker. It was clear I was never going to have an easy life in football. Jimmy Quinn came from Swindon. I'm pretty sure he scored against us in an FA Cup match with a big header. The trouble with Quinny was that he could never keep his concentration for a full match and, what made it worse, the fans knew it. He was a great header of the ball, had a potent right foot and for twenty minutes a game he was a fabulous player. But the rest of the time he'd just wander off into his own little world and it was like communicating with a Martian.

We'd become a very tight unit under Bobby and while there wasn't much flair in the side, we played to our strengths and understood our weaknesses. We had no loners or superstars who stood apart from anyone else. With Blackburn Rovers there were no airs or graces during that era, everyone worked together and Bobby led by example.

Though it has to be said he possibly took it a bit far sometimes. I'm sure he was just trying to be a part of the team and show he could muck in with the lads - and demonstrate just how tight cash was at the time - but I thought he was going to drown at Pleasington during training one morning. A miscued shot had cleared everyone's head and flew into the River Darwen, which runs through Blackburn and cuts through the playing fields. Anyone who knows it will agree that this is a particularly revolting section of the waterways of Lancashire. It's filthy, strewn with rubbish and home to more rats and other vermin than I'd like to dwell on. Even the pub players who use the pitches are reluctant to rescue a ball from those murky waters. Not Bobby. He scampered off in pursuit, got downstream of the ball and crouched on the bank to grab the ball as it passed him. It was inevitable what would follow and it was one of those wish-I-had-a-camcorder moments as he lost his footing and then toppled forwards into the blackness. He started screaming for help and someone - not me - jumped in to rescue him. His dog, a Yorkshire Terrier, also dived in to offer canine assistance. And all for a bloody knackered old ball. Still, we got the rest of the day off - we were laughing too hard to carry on training.

Up until Christmas we were in pretty unstoppable form, having reversed the fortunes of the end of the previous season. We played at Carlisle and Derek Fazackerley scored a penalty to put us four points clear at the top. It was some position to be in and we strengthened it with a 2-1 win over Leeds on Boxing Day. But then it started to go horribly wrong. Again. Huddersfield beat us at home and we lost to Manchester United in the FA Cup on a pitch as hard as the plastic at Loftus Road. But it's hard to place blame for the slip-up and I really don't know what else Bobby could have done. There wasn't the money to strengthen the squad and while the fans may have thought otherwise, we certainly didn't need a star name - the dressing-room atmosphere was magnificent and to have upset that would have made a big signing almost pointless and probably counter-productive at that time. It also seemed to me that it was impossible to find players at a reasonable price who might have improved the squad we had. All of which left us lacking a bit of sparkle, and by the end of the season that finally took its toll. We needed to win three or four of our last six games to go up but we blew it. Even on the last day of the season we still had a mathematical chance of going up when we played Wolves. Tommy Docherty, their manager at the time, came into our dressing room just before kick-off and sat in on Bobby's team talk, something I'd never seen before and certainly never saw again. In fact, I've no idea why Bobby let him in.

"Don't worry about our lot. We're crap."

He was right, but we also needed Manchester City and Portsmouth to lose but, inevitably, it didn't work out. We finished fifth. It was a nightmare. Each season we were getting better and up until Christmas we would be something like ten games from promotion and doing fine. Come the end of the season, we were still stuck in Division Two. Yet I still refuse to accept that it was beyond us. I was young and though it was heart-breaking I always felt there'd be another chance around the corner.

I'm an optimist by nature, which is why I've always been happy and secure in myself even when I was in prison. I'm optimistic about everything and I always think there'll be an answer to any tricky situation. I think it's a footballer thing because whatever else is going on in the world or in your life, your mind is locked into a brief period on a Saturday afternoon. You might be in debt, your marriage might be breaking down, you might have lost someone close. It doesn't matter. Because for those ninety minutes you're in front of 3,000 or 30,000 or any number of people and your job is to give them a lift, give them their week's pleasure. They're with you all the way and you can help their problems evaporate for a few minutes. And you do this week-in, week-out. If you weren't an optimist you'd realise how daft it all is...

5

STRUGGLING
1985 to 1986

...AND IT DOESN'T GET much dafter than going from being one of the top teams in the division to very nearly being relegated. The money had clearly dried up again because there was no incoming movement on the transfer front of any note pre-season.

Christmas came early in 1985. Not that that was good news for Blackburn Rovers, it simply meant our annual run of rubbish football started sooner than anticipated. After being unbeaten in our first half-dozen games we went something like ten games without a single victory. I had no doubt we were going down. That wasn't a lack of optimism, it was good old-fashioned honesty. It was getting desperate. We lost five games on the trot at home and then, completely out of nowhere, we stuck six past Sheffield United. I got the first after about thirty seconds. Dusty got into the box, pulled it back and I stuffed it in from the edge of the area. It was that game even more than the last of the season against Grimsby that kept us up. Our confidence was in ribbons, though none of us could believe we were playing so poorly, and to score six gave us a chance. Against Grimsby I scored early again, after about forty seconds, and we scraped through to stay up. That was my hundredth goal as a professional and one of the most important of my career. Quite honestly I had no idea. I know it's a cliché, but there was only one thing on my mind - win and we stay up, lose and...

STRUGGLING

...And the trouble is, I can't get close to explaining why it all went so wrong. Our team was ageing so perhaps there wasn't the same consistency in team selection, but we had good younger players coming through and we were pretty fit. It wasn't as if we were getting bored with Bobby's style, we weren't. Everyone stuck together and we did our best. It just wasn't good enough and we weren't good enough. But the loyalty the team showed Bobby never faltered. He had a great way with players and knew how everyone ticked as individuals as well as a team. He dropped me for a game against Leeds United but I came out of his office feeling like I'd just had a pay rise.

"Look Simon, you're not playing tomorrow, you need a rest, but I guarantee you'll be playing the next game."

He was true to his word. Five minutes with Bobby and the world was a wonderful place again. Not that the fans saw any of that though. Bobby was a reserved and shy man in public. He said his piece in the dressing room and at the training ground. But put a microphone in front of him and he didn't want to know. He could have done with someone to talk to the media for him, because it was his only real weakness.

It was a simple philosophy that Bobby put in place, it had to be. We were skint so he had to have players who could slot in and out of a hard-working unit. In football you can function reasonably if eight of the starting line-up are on top of their game - the other three can be carried. Bobby's line was that if those three gave 100% in terms of effort then he was satisfied. Any less than that and he'd make his feelings known. In private. Always in private. That's how the loyalty developed.

It was around that time I saw another approach to man-management in the game, or rather boy-management. John, who was about six by now, was playing for Blue Star FC in

Blackburn. I was a bit of a local celebrity which made it difficult for me watching the games because I could never really shout encouragement in case I was seen to be a smart arse. But the other dads?

"Come on Kevin, use it, USE IT, oh bloody hell ref, REF!"

And on and on and on. All the frustrations of these dads - who would have loved to have been in my shoes - just pouring out from the touchline. Bloody hell, they were worse than the moaners on the Riverside.

At least it gave me the chance to meet people from the area who weren't directly connected with football, people like Bob Dickinson, a car dealer, Andy McKie, who I later went into business with, and Big Jim Kelly from Darwen. They were mostly fans as well, so these guys became regular drinking buddies in the 100 Club after games. In those days most of the players would socialise with fans. Some would leave after a quick half if they had distances to travel but me . . . I'd stay until the world had been put to rights. Which was usually about closing time.

The summer of 1986 saw Bobby make two of the best signings in my time at Blackburn, not that it did us much good. Chris Price came from Hereford and Scott Sellars from Leeds, where he'd been struggling to make an impression. Chris gave us a new dimension because he was always keen to get forward from his right-back position. He also added a new dimension to my social life because he liked a drink. Chris was another typical Bobby signing in that nobody had ever heard of him, but he settled in straight away. And the fans loved him because his work and scoring rate was unbelievable. Jim Branagan, who Chris effectively replaced, was a fine, steady footballer, but never went over the half-way line whereas Chris was a throw-back to the Kevin Hird days - a full-back who was adventurous and gave the fans something to cheer.

STRUGGLING

As for Scott, he had the best left foot I've ever had the pleasure to be on the park with. His right foot was useless, mind. My baby has a better right peg. But that left was so sweet. Scott was light as a feather and wasn't exactly blessed with great pace but he could walk past a player and cross brilliantly. With Simon Barker inside him in the midfield we had the making of a phenomenal team. The best thing about Scott was that he was always a team player. He'd won some England Under-23 caps but was nothing other than absolutely down-to-earth. He was also first to put his hand in the air at the suggestion of a beer and he was a glorious piss-taker and wind-up merchant. Anyone who tried it on with him was quickly cut down to size. The trouble was, you could never really get him back because he was too quick with his mouth and too clever with the ball, which was fine on match day but infuriating in training

Unfortunately, the qualities Chris and Scott brought didn't really help much, certainly not in terms of the league. The fans were really on our backs and Quinny caught most of it which, again, got me off the hook. What fans want to see is players giving 100% all the time. They'll forgive you if things aren't working out if it looks like you're breaking your back for the cause but Jimmy never even looked enthusiastic enough to break wind. The fans got to him and he became increasingly withdrawn and depressed by the situation. Even if he'd scored six goals in a game the fans would have booed him for missing a half-chance. Rather than trying to nurture him and help him out of the hole, Bobby decided to let Jimmy go back to Swindon in an effort to let him rescue his career. It worked, but it was a first sign that Bobby's judgement was becoming suspect. The signing of Paul McKinnon, a non-league player from

Sutton, just before Christmas was the second sign and effectively sealed the manager's fate. It was a desperate move to try and counter a desperate situation. With one awful season behind us, another was now staring us in the face and we were heading for the drop again. If the fans thought McKinnon was a surprise signing, imagine how we felt. For the first time players were losing confidence in Bobby's decisions - not Bobby himself, just his response to a difficult time. His judgement was being swayed by panic. Yes, we were dying a death in the league, but Paul was not the answer. He worked hard and did his best but he just wasn't up to the job.

It had been another one of those seasons. We'd started reasonably well and I scored four against Sunderland, who were a decent team, but we went off the boil pretty soon after. By the time we next played them in December, when Paul made his debut, the train was off the rails and we were thumped 3-0. On Boxing Day we lost to Huddersfield when Duncan Shearer, who Kenny Dalglish later signed, scored. And then Bobby was sacked. The fans were happy but despite everything the players were devastated and we felt he deserved more time. In fact, we felt he'd earned a right to it. Jim Branagan was club captain at the time and before the board meeting which saw Bobby fired he organised a petition among the players to tell the directors how strongly we felt about keeping him as manager. Not a single player refused to sign. We'd had a great run under Bobby. He'd spent something like £350,000 on players during his time at Ewood and recouped about half a million. He'd kept us happy on fairly modest wages and by and large we'd done well. He stood by us when we were getting stick and never once blamed a player in public for the problems.

STRUGGLING

Jim pushed the petition under the door at the meeting but it made no difference. He was gone. We had a dinner for him at the Red House Motel and every player attended and drank his health.

In retrospect Bobby made some mistakes towards the end. We were an ageing team and he stuck by players he maybe should have let go earlier. That said, how was he going to replace them? There was still no sign of any cash to strengthen the squad. And anyway, it wasn't Bobby who was on the pitch playing crap - it was us. Me included, though not for the first time my man-of-the-people image shielded me from the more vociferous supporters who diverted their attentions elsewhere. I was viewed as someone from the terraces who'd come good, and I never had any problems being with fans. I loved it and still like being recognised and talked to. I'd autograph anything for anybody and try to help out wherever possible. At away games you'd get fans who'd travelled hundreds of miles and they'd be on the scrounge for our complimentary tickets.

"Too right. Here you go sunshine."

They were paying my wages and if they wanted an autograph or my help with a ticket then it was the least I could do. As for wages, we didn't do too badly, despite the fact we were neither a rich nor a particularly successful club in those days. I'd be a liar if I said I wouldn't have minded being better paid, and I can only guess what my salary would be if I'd been in my prime at the turn of the Millennium, but I have no real gripes. At my earnings peak, which coincided with me leaving the club, I was making a basic of £600 a week, which translates to something like £30,000 a year - certainly not to be sniffed at, but hardly in the league of the modern player, even outside the Premiership. During Bobby's time I reached about £450 plus bonuses and, at Blackburn, there was an excellent system which was worth about £40 a point, or £120 a win. In comparison to our wages, it was a good top-up, and it didn't matter where we were in the league.

At a lot of clubs you had to be in a certain position in the league for the payments to kick in. With others it was an accumulating scheme so, for example, you'd get £50 for the first win, £100 for the second, £200 for the third and so on. But as soon as you lost a game you went back to the £50. Chris Woods, the ex-England keeper, had been a friend of mine since school days and when he was at Norwich they used this scheme. They played us after winning seven consecutive games, the eighth would have provided a massive amount of cash. I scored twice and we beat them easily. Strangely enough, the drinks were on me that night!

The Bobby Saxton era was over. Seeing his name removed from the manager's door was like losing a close relative. Bobby had accepted a chalice of fire in taking over from Howard Kendall and had twice taken us to the brink of promotion. But in his final few weeks, when things were going horribly wrong for us again in the league, and, to be frank, the transfer market, he sowed the seeds for one of the great days of an otherwise barren era.

We'd started to make progress in the Full Members Cup. It was a something-or-nothing tournament which we hadn't even bothered to enter the previous season. About a dozen people turned up for the first match of this campaign and though it was vilified, I loved it. It was a mid-week game, which meant we didn't have to train too hard on a Tuesday morning. Instead of running round a field in the name of getting fit without a ball in sight, we could go and play for real. But once the new manager was in position, it became very serious indeed and effectively rescued the season.

6

WINNING
1987

TONY PARKES TOOK CONTROL after Bobby left, which was a tough assignment. The players had been right behind Bobby and it didn't matter who took over because there was always going to be something of an atmosphere as the new man - even in a caretaker role - would have to make changes to stop what was becoming a serious downward spiral. What Tony had in his favour was the fact the players had a great deal of respect for him. There was always an air about him that marked him out for a managerial or coaching position and, just like when he was a player, he always put all his energies into his job.

He got us off to a reasonable start and I think there were two things at play here. Firstly, we'd let ourselves and Bobby down and we knew we had to reverse what was a critical situation and, secondly, a new full-time manager would be in place soon and we'd have to impress on him that we were up for the fight or we might be on our way out.

Finally we were introduced to our new manager, Don Mackay. At risk of repeating myself - Don who? He came from a backroom job at Glasgow Rangers and he'd worked in Dundee and for Coventry, which was the sum total of our knowledge. Almost immediately we noticed the key difference between Don and Bobby. Where Bobby was calm, relaxed and shy in public, Don was brash, loud and confident almost to the point of being overwhelming. We learnt quickly that no matter how wrong he was about something he was still right. Training changed again and, particularly in the early days, it was very long and laborious work. He was in many ways quite arrogant about his approach to the game and would insist on doing things his way. Don't get me wrong, that's the job of a manager, but usually you expect some kind of input from the players. Not with Don.

Still, it brought results and we started to dig ourselves out of trouble in the league and, with the Full Members Cup as a good diversion, we started to achieve some kind of shape. Under Bobby we'd crept past Huddersfield in this most minor of cup contests and we'd done so by fielding a strong side. It was the same situation against Sheffield United - in front of a dismal crowd - and it was only after beating Oxford 4-3, when we'd been forced to come from behind, that people started to sit up and notice - not least the players. It was then we realised we weren't far from a trip to Wembley. Beating Chelsea in the quarter-final was a big deal. I was on the scoresheet and Sean Curry, who Tony had signed from Liverpool's reserves, got one. Then it was Ipswich in the semis.

Just before the game Glenn Keeley was ruled out for some reason and Don bolstered the defence with a pair of Scottish signings - Colin Hendry, who Don picked up for £30,000 from Dundee, and Chris Sulley. The Full Members Cup was the making of Colin and turned him into a Blackburn legend. If Bobby knew the south-west, Scotland was definitely Don's patch. He really knew the scene. Despite the fact he was a complete unknown and little more than a fresh-faced kid, Colin walked in like he owned the place. He had a presence which could be recognised instantly. Not quite cocky, but brimming with confidence about his abilities which, to be frank, were modest to begin with. His attitude reminded me of John Radford, but John had an FA Cup winner's medal whereas Colin just had a posture, an attitude and a memorable haircut. In the dressing-room, right from day one, he had plenty to say. Even Glenn was a bit taken aback, and he had the biggest mouth of anyone. A few of the more experienced players found him a pain in the arse. After all, he'd come for a few pennies from Dundee United but talked as though he was a regular in a championship side. And he always fancied himself more as a striker than a defender, which Don certainly never had in mind and wasn't something I wanted to dwell on too much - Blackburn had bought and sold enough strikers to man a picket-line since my debut. But Colin was Colin and as he matured he became one of Don's and the club's greatest assets. As a defender.

That certainly took a while to get into his head. He was forever getting forward, regardless of the holes he left at the back, and his only objective in every game, or so it seemed, was to break forward and score a goal. The fans loved it, but it left us exposed and made us vulnerable to counter-attacks. He'd try to dribble past three or four players from the edge of our box and while it must have been exciting to watch it left the rest of us a bag of nerves. It took the team a while to adjust to his style but Don obviously - and rightly as it turned out - saw the potential. It didn't seem like it when he first arrived, but Colin was a very intelligent player. He'd go on these runs and leave his position, but we very rarely suffered from his actions. He timed things well and never more so than at Wembley for the final.

First though, we had to get past Ipswich in the semi, another home draw. The players, fans and local media were now really up for the tournament. I'd like to say we were taking each match as it came but it would be a lie. Under Don we'd got ourselves out of trouble in the league, which was an enormous relief, and found some breathing space. The only thing I was thinking about was the possibility of appearing at Wembley and there's no doubt we coasted through the odd league match. This might have been a once-in-a-lifetime opportunity.

That night against Ipswich went by in a blur. My only memories are of winning a penalty and being accused of diving, which I didn't, and scoring a goal from open play. The ball came to me from the right wing and I blasted it in to the near post from about twelve yards. It was a sweet shot but there was a late blocking challenge as I struck it and I cracked the bottom of the defender's boot. I was in agony but there was no way I wasn't going to celebrate this one - on the pitch or over a pint or dozen afterwards. Despite the fact it was largely Bobby's team who'd got us to Wembley, Don, who'd been at the club for five minutes, just couldn't help himself.

"I've got this team to Wembley for the first time in years . . ."

He loved talking to the media. To be honest he loved talking to anyone who'd listen. Fair enough, he was trying to boost the profile of Blackburn Rovers, but eventually he started to think he owned the bloody place. He wanted an input into all aspects of the club and he was an expert at everything from how many tea bags were needed for the perfect brew to which soap powder should be used on the kit.

The final was less than three weeks away, a first Wembley appearance for Blackburn in nearly three decades, and it never left the back of my mind. I don't care what anyone says but when there was a fifty-fifty challenge in those games leading up to the final, I was a bit wary. Nobody wanted to miss out and I wasn't going to put my place at Wembley at risk by gambling on a tackle in a meaningless league game. It's the only time in my career when I deliberately under-performed. Don might have been a big-gob and he might have been conceited and arrogant, but he was no fool. This game was as important to him as it was to us and he knew his reputation and standing could be bolstered forever if we won. Training eased off and we concentrated as much on staying calm and killing the nerves as organising tactics. It wasn't easy. Regardless of all the promotional close-calls and regardless of the fact there was no European place at stake, this was still the biggest game of our careers and we might never get another shot at something so exciting - in the grand scheme of things very few players get the chance to play at Wembley. I'd never even been there as a spectator.

We got to our base a couple of days before the game and it was very, very boring. There was so little to do and we certainly couldn't have a drink to numb the tension. Under a different manager that may not have been the case, but even I felt it was the right thing to do. We'd train in the mornings and use the gym or the pool to while away the afternoons. Or some of the lads did. I ended up spending most of my time in the snooker room. We'd have a communal dinner in the evening and by ten o'clock there was nothing to do but get into bed and try and get some sleep. That wasn't easy either.

The nerves really started to build when we left the hotel on the day of the game. We had a police escort, which made us feel like real stars, and as we started to see the fans as we got closer to the stadium the butterflies turned into rampant eagles. I don't get unsettled easily and I'd always been relaxed going into games but this was different. This was scary.

THERE'S ONLY ONE SIMON GARNER

And here's the thing. You get out on to the pitch and it all looks wonderful. The changing rooms were fantastic, the stands look superb, but the pitch itself? Dreadful. On the television it always looked so good with its crisp lawnmower lines, but underfoot it was terrible. The turf was patchy, uneven, and pitted. Who says the camera never lies?

"This game isn't going to pass me by. This game isn't going to pass me by. This game . . ."

The game passed me by.

I know it was a poor match, all stop-start, and that we had very few shots. I know that Vince O'Keefe emerged from the shadows, overcame his awful nerves and played a blinder in our goal. I know our fans outnumbered the Charlton fans massively - we had about 30,000 there. The only other thing I really remember is there were about five minutes to go when Alan Ainscow played Ian Miller in on the right wing. He beat a defender and I was screaming for a ball to the near post but he knocked it straight over my head. I think Bob Bolder got a touch on it but it fell for Colin, who was partnering me up front, and he smacked it in off the post. No wonder he fancied himself as a striker; it was a superb effort.

The feeling was incredible. I can't imagine what it's like to lose at Wembley after all the sweat that goes in to getting there. Nobody remembers the team who comes second. I played there another three times and was never on the losing side. You just don't want to leave the pitch. That's what being a professional is all about - going to the spiritual home of the game and winning. It's what the years of perseverance and disappointments are all for. You do a lap of honour and you want to do it again. And again. And again. Throughout my career I'd always been first off the pitch at the final whistle, straight into the bath and then off to the bar for a pint and a fag. Not at Wembley. That's how good it was.

Don was ecstatic. It was the pinnacle of his career. And though I think a lot of the players had thoughts of Bobby in the backs of their minds, who knows what might have happened if Bobby had stayed? It certainly looked like we might go down and I suspect the Full Members Cup would have been given a lesser priority. And in fairness to Don, he picked the team and his player scored the goal. I know a lot of fans would have liked Bobby to have been at Wembley in some capacity, but that's not the way football is or should be - you have to look forward, not backwards. They say you're only as good as your last game, but in reality it's the next that really counts.

Playing at Wembley was utterly exhausting. It wasn't the size of the pitch, which wasn't that big anyway, and it wasn't the fact the turf was so mediocre. It was simply the occasion. The build-up and the tension eventually gets to you and to hear the final whistle - having won - was an immense relief.

"You didn't play very well, did you?"

Then he burst out laughing. My dad was absolutely made up about us winning. He was right, I didn't play well, but I'd won a cup. And I'd won it at Wembley. We celebrated in fine fashion. In the players' bar at Wembley I just drank anything in front of me. The journey home was even more of a blur than the game. And the civic reception, which was a brilliant occasion, was really only remembered through photographs! It looked like the same 30,000 who'd been with us to Wembley the day before had descended on the town hall in Blackburn. I was drunk with beer and emotion, and I know there were thousands of others who shared the hangover.

THERE'S ONLY ONE SIMON GARNER

The rest of the season came and went. We could never beat the feeling of Wembley and I think we were glad when the summer break came. Safe in the middle of the table but, judging by our efforts in the Full Members, plenty to look forward to.

7

RECORD-BREAKING
1987 to 1989

THE FULL MEMBERS CUP was a great achievement despite it having virtually no prestige attached to it, but it was the league where we needed to perform. Don was settling in and starting to shape the team. He brought Ally Dawson down from Rangers and he slotted straight in. While he wasn't well-known he was an international player and we didn't have too many of those at Blackburn. If he was a steady, solid player, the same could hardly be said of Howard Gayle.

Don signed him from Stoke but Howard had seen the bright lights at Birmingham and during his time with Liverpool. He had a reputation for being a big-time charlie and an equally big drinker. He wound up some of the players because he had an opinion about everything and liked the sound of his own voice, but I got on well enough with him. He was good to have around the place because he'd perk people up and make them laugh. But the tales of his excessive drinking habits seemed some way off the mark - he was a lightweight! Importantly though, the fans loved him even if his form was erratic to say the least. It didn't matter how he was playing, he'd try and gee the crowd up like some kind of cheerleader.

Even so, it was a risky signing. And a brave one. If you're from the school of thought that says you only buy to improve what you already have, then you have to wonder if it was a good deal. Nicky Reid on the other hand was a sure-fire good bit of business. He was just the sort of player Don liked because he'd run for 120 minutes a game - I mean it. He'd be running before kick-off non-stop and he'd be running on the spot in the dressing-room after the final whistle. I roomed with Nicky for a while, which made for an interesting mix. On away trips he'd be up way too early to go stretching, walking and warming-up. I'd roll into the dining room as late as I could get away with.

Nicky wasn't the best footballer in the world but he was brought in to do a job and he played that midfield holding role extremely well. He was never a fan's favourite - steady players rarely are - but he'd get stuck in, get the ball and give it to someone who could play a bit. Don made him club captain and he was a good choice. He'd played most of his career at Manchester City and the players had a lot of respect for his achievements. He was also a natural leader, something we needed to help steady our nerve and steel our resolve.

We had another slow start to the season but we then went on a fantastic run of twenty-three games unbeaten and, for the hundredth time in my career, or so it seemed, we were top of Division Two and in the driving seat for promotion. Then Don pulled off two of the most remarkable signings in the history of the club. First he brought in Steve Archibald from Barcelona and then trumped that with the unveiling of Ossie Ardiles, a World Cup winner with Argentina and a world-class player.

Bloody hell's bells was the general response to Steve's signing. The attendances nearly doubled and suddenly great things were expected of us. We'd known absolutely nothing about it but we did know that he must have been on a fair old wedge. We didn't mind that - he was a massive name and put bums on seats. I think, in part, it suited the image Don wanted to give of himself - as a major operator who could claim credit for these amazing signings.

Steve was under a lot of pressure. He'd done everything at Tottenham and done reasonably at Barcelona. Not only did he have to perform to the level of his reputation, he also had to put himself in the shop-window at a lower league club. This was a loan signing that gave Steve the chance of first team football and time to sort out his next big move. His attitude was similar to that of a lot of modern players - he'd play the game then get straight home. He didn't really mix with the others and just got on with his job. That was difficult for me because here was someone, like John Radford, I felt I could learn from but because he said so little it was hard to get close enough.

Ossie became a good friend, partly I'm sure because he was a smoker and card-player! As a player he was superb but he picked up a nasty knock from future Rover Nicky Marker so Blackburn fans only saw him play half-a-dozen games. The other reason I have such a soft-spot for him is that when he went on to management, he was the one who offered me another chance of regular first team football.

Despite the stars around the club, the wheels started to come off in March and were rolling down the hill by Easter. We'd now slipped out of contention for automatic promotion and we were clinging to the hope of the play-offs. Throughout it all we retained our composure and while results were poor the tension rarely showed. It was never more so than when we had to visit Millwall in the final game of the season and, to be sure of the play-offs, we needed to win. It was a tricky game to call in advance because they had already been promoted and so it could either turn out to be their season's swan-song or, with luck, they'd ease off the gas. Either way, it would still be a difficult night because the Den was a frightening place to play due to some incredibly aggressive fans. I scored twice as we won 4-1. Whoops - there was a pitch invasion as soon as the game finished. It was a little bit hairy! When the whistle went we were attacking in the furthest place on the pitch from the tunnel and I simply legged it off the park. Nicky Reid was the last to appear in the dressing room - he'd been carried off by two policemen after being swallowed up by this mass of Londoners - and the only item of clothing he had left on was his jockstrap. Thank God they'd already been promoted; the invasion was as near to a friendly atmosphere as you're likely to get at Millwall.

We were now in a four-way tussle but we crumbled at the first hurdle. Chelsea, who had finished bottom of Division One and were obliged to take part, took us to pieces and showed that while we had a decent enough team to compete in Division Two we really didn't have the class even to get beyond the worst side in the top flight. I've never considered the play-offs a just means of deciding promotion, but that didn't mean I wasn't going to give my all to help us through them. But it counted for nothing. In the first round they beat us 2-0 at Ewood and 4-1 at Stamford Bridge. In reality they gave us a good pasting and killed what was a promising and, for a while, a rather glamorous season.

Being my testimonial season, it's a shame we couldn't cap it off with promotion. I enjoyed the testimonial which was offered in recognition of ten years service at the club. It was enormously important to me financially because while I was earning what would be considered a good salary, it would be nothing compared to riches available these days. From my perspective, I saw it as a kind of compensation for the fact I was never transferred and so never made anything from signing-on fees.

My testimonial committee was a great bunch and included Richard Matthewman, who is now the club's vice-chairman, and Alan Cotton, who was the testimonial chairman, someone I knew from the 100-Club, and he'd run a testimonial season before, so it was good to have him on board. Paul Schofield, a solicitor and another of the 100-Club crowd, was secretary. Andy McKie, who became a business associate with me with the Rococo shop, partly funded by the proceeds of the year, was also in the team.

While the main event was the testimonial game, there were other occasions like a golf day and dinner dances where a few quid could be made, and then there were pool and darts nights in the pubs, which I really enjoyed - free beer and fags, and I get paid at the end of it!

My game was against Newcastle, who had approached the club about a pre-season friendly, and the attendance was excellent - around 7,000, which was about the size of the crowds we were pulling then. Over the season I made £32,000, which doesn't seem a lot now but to me it was good money. More to the point, it had been a lot of fun.

You get to wonder if it was some kind of subconscious complacency - we knew we were good enough to be promoted but we also knew there was the safety net of the play-offs. It was a feeling we were going to get used to.

We lost a lot of players that summer. The loan spells for Ossie and Steve had run their course, Chris Price went to Villa, Simon Barker to Queen's Park Rangers. And it wasn't as if these guys were bit-part players, they were all first team regulars and major contributors to the cause. I can imagine the fans thinking we were going back to the bad old days when we sold to survive.

THERE'S ONLY ONE SIMON GARNER

That summer's influx hardly inspired. Tony Finnigan was brought from relative obscurity at Crystal Palace. He never really settled at Blackburn, mainly because he was a London-boy, a Flash-Harry and always a wheeler-dealer. He was a good laugh who showed good promise on the pitch but faded quickly.

Ronnie Hildersley was a big boost in the dressing room even though he was the smallest player in the league at the time. If we lost a game 4-0, Ronnie could have us giggling and relaxed enough for the next game. And he was a good player too. He never ducked a challenge, played a good passing game and scored a few goals.

Mark Atkins also came in as a replacement for Chris Price and he became one of the most under-rated performers I've ever played with. While his skills were limited, he was an intelligent, industrious player who understood his strengths. The fans were too quick to see his shortcomings but when Blackburn won the title in 1995, I felt he was a key man in the campaign.

And then there was Andy Kennedy - a legend in his own trousers. No-one knew how to take to him. He walked into the dressing room expecting us to ooh and aah and offer to clean his boots. It's just as well he knew how ridiculous he seemed to other people. He liked to have a good time and it was infectious. The sad thing about Andy is that he never got close to fulfilling his potential. He could have been a massive star but never had the discipline to make the most of his talents. He was very quick, though never looked it, and could hit a ball with incredible power and accuracy. But because he would never put the extra mile in, he was utterly inconsistent. Women loved him, and he was consistent enough about that area of his life. He dated Maria Whittaker when she was the hot Page

RECORD-BREAKING

Three model, but he was a lad who was never going to settle down and he lived up to the reputation of being a professional footballer.

It seemed an unusual bunch to bring to Blackburn but, despite losing some of our best players, we nonetheless had a strong season as the team began to gel.

I also had the biggest day of my career, which also turned out to be one of the worst in the history of the game. April 15, 1989 is rightly remembered for one thing - the Hillsborough disaster. We knew something had happened but we had no concept of how awful it was. My mind had been concentrated on the fact I was close to breaking the all-time scoring record at Blackburn, held by Tommy Briggs. I hadn't scored for ages but I knew I only needed two goals to break the record. The match was against Manchester City, who were top of the table, and we beat them 4-0. I scored a lucky goal in the first half. I think somebody had a shot which came back off the post for a tap-in. The second was a belter. I cracked it left-footed at the Blackburn End into the far corner past Paul Cooper. That was the record-breaker and the hat-trick goal wasn't bad either - I turned into the area and scored off the post. I don't think the record will ever be broken, not the way players move on so much these days, and it's something I'm immensely proud of. In fact, I was quite pleased when Alan Shearer left for Newcastle - he was catching up too quickly!

So there I was, the greatest scorer in the history of the club. OK so I never got a £1m move to Manchester United but I did something good at Blackburn Rovers that people will always remember. That's important to me. Even at the time I knew I was trying to give something to the fans to remember me by - not just the drinking and the fags - but the goals.

THERE'S ONLY ONE SIMON GARNER

I think it was Gary Newbon from ITV who collared me at the side of the pitch for an interview.

"How did it feel to break the record?"

"I'm knackered."

That's all I could say because it's exactly how I felt. The scale of Hillsborough became apparent after the game when I was in the 100 Club. There's so much been said and written about Hillsborough and there's not much I can add. I only know that football isn't worth even one death.

We finished a creditable fifth and squared up to Watford in the first leg of the play-off semi-final. It was a scrappy game which finished 0-0 and I had a running battle with their centre-half Paul Miller. I never considered myself a dirty player and I never got into too much trouble on the pitch, but enough was enough and he'd been mouthing off through the whole game. They got a goal-kick and as we jogged back to the middle of the pitch together I took a look at the referee and the linesmen, saw they were looking the other way, and whacked him. I caught him right across the face and he went down like a sack of spuds. Then I jogged away looking the picture of innocence.

In the second leg, at Watford, I scored with my first touch of the game and we drew 1-1 to go through thanks to the away goal. As the game wore on they were getting more and more frustrated. I was chasing a long ball over the top with Miller as my marker and he got his revenge for the Ewood spat when he turned round and smacked me one. But I had the last laugh. He was spotted and sent-off.

We'd been in the play-offs before and we felt good about the home and away final against Crystal Palace. It was a strange game, the one at home. Howard Gayle scored two and then missed a penalty. They came back with one and I scored a late goal. A 3-1 lead should have been enough for a team as well-organised and disciplined as ours. I was rooming with Scott Sellars on the night before the game and I don't think either of us slept a wink. We just kept spinning it round our heads and talking about how this was the best chance we'd ever get.

The Selhurst Park leg was a disaster. With the exception of the Full Members Cup Final, it was the only time in my career that I felt genuinely nervous before a game. Every Blackburn fan knows, and I'm pretty sure most Palace fans would admit, that referee George bloody Courtney had a nightmare. There was definitely a foul by Colin Hendry but it was definitely outside the box. And the penalty definitely cost us a place in the top flight. When we were 2-0 down I hit this shot from twenty yards, the sweetest volley of my life, and I could see it flying into the top corner and I could see me running out at Old Trafford and then I could see the keeper make the most incredible save. And I think I knew then that it wasn't our day. We conceded a third in extra-time, most of which we played with thousands of Palace fans encroaching on to the pitch. Courtney should have stopped the game and insist they move back.

When the whistle went and I had finally fought my way to the tunnel I just sat down and started crying. I really thought we were there this time, that we'd finally laid to rest the hoodoo. Ian Wright, who partnered Mark Bright in an awesome forward line, put an arm round me.

"Hard luck."

He meant it and it meant a lot to me. Wright was a brilliant player who put so much work into his game. I know he's remembered for his goals, particularly when he was at Arsenal, but his off-the-ball work was excellent as well. I'd love to have played with him because he was so generous. Years later, when I was at Wycombe, we watched an Ian Wright video on the way to the play-off final for inspiration. I'd have paid to watch him, though obviously not when he moved to Burnley!

8

CHANGING
1989 to 1991

SO BACK TO THE DRAWING-BOARD again. Don worked hard in the transfer market and picked up Frank Stapleton from Le Havre and Kevin Moran from Sporting Gijon. These guys were legends. They were both coming towards the ends of their careers but there's no doubting the boost it gave us after the disappointment of the play-offs - and the fact that Colin Hendry left for Manchester City. Frank had a big reputation in the game. He'd done everything at Manchester United and Arsenal and was a class act. But there were no pretensions at all. He always had time to talk and his advice was devoured, and he was brilliant to play with because he was a team player who always gave his all. And the same is true of Kevin. He had cuts, bruises and scars all over the place and never shirked a challenge. They'd travel to games together and Frank nearly always drove because Kevin's reputation for liking a beer after the game is well-earned.

Losing Colin was a blow, certainly from a playing perspective. The way the players saw it was that his dad, who'd been a driving instructor I think, had effectively become his agent and saw better things ahead for Colin. Not everyone in the dressing-room was upset though, far from it in fact. He was a good player and clearly ambitious but there was a feeling he was getting too big for his boots and that Blackburn was somehow not good enough for him any more. When he left a second time for Glasgow Rangers, when Blackburn were struggling again, I couldn't help feeling a sense of déjà vu. The days of loyalty are over. No further comment required.

On the positive side we had Keith Hill and David May coming through the ranks in defensive positions. They were both very promising and it's a compliment to the club's youth system that they were strong enough to be considered ready to break into the first team. It's always been an impressive set-up, especially when you think about the competition within thirty or forty miles of Blackburn - the Merseyside and Manchester clubs are all looking for the best young talent too.

My judgement has never been the best but I think most people expected Keith to emerge as the better player. Since their times at Blackburn they've both had good careers but for Keith it was with the likes of Plymouth and Rochdale while David played a part in winning the Champions League for Manchester United.

Frankly it wasn't a vintage season. We had good young players like Lenny Johnrose, Craig Skinner and Darren Collier to call on, but they didn't seem to offer us much depth. And here's another example of my famous talent-spotting abilities. Later, when I was at West Brom, we played Plymouth and Peter Shilton was player-manager. We went up for a ball together and he smacked two of my teeth out. He rang me up the next day and I thought he was calling to apologise. He wasn't. But I had the last laugh, even if it was by accident.

"I've been looking at a couple of your former team-mates and I wonder if you could give me your thoughts on Jason Wilcox and Craig Skinner."

"Well, if it was me, I'd go for Craig."

I genuinely felt he was the better prospect. He seemed to have a better all-round game and awareness. And so Shilts bought him. Craig moved sideways in the lower leagues while Jason played for England and Leeds and lifted the title with Blackburn. And people still ask me why I didn't go into coaching or management.

Despite us never really getting into our stride we still made the play-offs - for the third season in succession. Ossie Ardiles was then manager at Swindon, who we played in the semi-final. We lost the first leg 2-1 at home and Don dropped me for the away match to play Frank up front on his own. I didn't understand that idea at all, we needed to score goals. I saw Ossie before the game for a natter. He reached into the fridge and grabbed a can of beer.

"Drink Simon?"

"I can't, Ossie, I'm on the bench."

"Go on, share a can with me."

"Yeah, go on."

It was only half a can, maybe I should have had a crate. We lost 2-1 again and I barely had a touch for the time I was on. Swindon eventually got promoted but didn't kick a ball in the top flight because they were stung for financial irregularities before Ossie's time. There was an argument, mainly coming from the supporters, that we should be allowed a second chance because Swindon, by the due process of fan logic, should not have taken part in the play-offs. Despite the fact we'd missed out three times in the play-offs, it wasn't a view I held. We didn't go up because we weren't good enough. End of story. And while it was devastating to have come so close again I can barely imagine how the Swindon players felt after thinking they'd made it.

It was around this time that the media started talking about us being the 'nearly-men' of football. It was fair comment, of course, having come so close on so many occasions in the past decade. We were also getting a name for being every fan's second favourite club - Burnley fans excepted. It was because of the club's history I suppose, and the romanticism attached to having won the FA Cup six times, three of those in successive years. They might have been well-meant words and intentions but the players hated it. We didn't want to be nearly-men and we didn't give a tuppence about being liked by other fans. We wanted to win. We wanted to prove that we could do it. But we didn't realise how soon that was going to happen and how much things were about to change.

9

RECUPERATING
1990 to 1991

DON'S LAST FULL SEASON was a let-down in playing terms for all involved, not least for me as it was the first time in my career that I picked up a serious injury - a double hernia caused, more than likely, by general wear and tear. Don tried to bolster the squad and Lee Richardson was a good signing. He came to us from Watford in a swap deal for Andy Kennedy. He was a classy player and a cheeky bugger. He'd call me dad on away trips, especially when we were pissed which was probably a little too often. The way the deal worked meant he was valued at £60,000 which was an absolute bargain. He had a lot of skill but did more in games than the fans gave him credit for and even if the magic wasn't there he'd still put the effort in.

Mick Duxbury came in too. He was another Manchester United veteran but not from the same mould as Kevin Moran - Mick was a quiet bloke who'd get back to his allotment to tend to his vegetable patch as soon as training was finished.

For most of the season I was a spectator. The club specialist told me my hernia problem was probably not worth operating on because I was coming to the end of my career. Scott Sellars had a similar problem at the same time and he was told he didn't need an operation at all. We both decided to get second opinions - I felt, at thirty, that I had a lot more football left in me and retirement was the last thing I wanted to contemplate, while Scott thought he had a serious problem that needed sorting out.

We took the right decisions in insisting on second opinions, but the pain was only just worth it. We went to a private clinic in Yorkshire and were given hernia tests where the doctor pushed a finger right into the groin. The agony was indescribable and when he told me he was going to test the other side too I was ready to jump off the couch and run home. Sadly, the fact I could only hobble wrecked this plan. We'd taken the initiative ourselves for the second opinion but reported back to Bill Fox, the chairman, telling him we needed operations. There was some dispute over our results and Jack Cunningham, the club physio, was backing the club specialist's opinion but Bill over-ruled and stumped up the cash.

We went together to a private hospital in Manchester and had a week of being pampered. But it was hard work, especially when you needed to laugh. I had twenty-two staples on each side of my groin which, as you can imagine, was not comfortable. We were watching LA Law from our beds one night and it was painfully funny, in the most literal sense. We eventually had to turn it off. On the sixth day they wanted to know if we'd managed, as they put it, to open our bowels. No problem for Scott but I'd been somewhat reluctant.

"So, you haven't been at all then Simon?"

"Erm, no. Sorry."

"Well we'll have to give you a suppository then."

I groaned. At least having my groin poked only felt like having a poker shoved up the rear; this time it was for real. Then a young, attractive nurse popped into the room. Could be worse, I thought, until she sloped off to be replaced by some burly male nurse wearing rubber gloves and an evil grin. That was not a pleasant experience and nor was our rehabilitation, which was ridiculously drawn out. At the time players at other clubs who were being seen by sports specialists were getting back into action within a few weeks, but we were more-or-less planning our own programmes. And that involved lots and lots of cycling. The only benefit of this solitary struggle for fitness was that it took me past, or rather into, some of East Lancashire's more out-of-the-way hostelries.

By the time I returned we were down at the bottom of the table and struggling, though we were unlucky not to beat Liverpool in the FA Cup. I'd put us a goal up but right at the end of the game Mark Atkins scored an own-goal. If that wasn't bad enough for him, Jimmy Hill immortalised the incident on Match of the Day when he tried to blame the ball-girl for giving the ball to a Liverpool player too quickly. Kenny Dalglish was manager and this was the start of the cup run which eventually led to him resigning after the Everton game.

In the league it was getting desperate. We had a terrible run of injuries and Don was scrabbling round the loan market for players to do a short-term job, but it wasn't working out. After three years in the play-offs and a cup at Wembley, we were looking ripe for relegation. And then came Jack Walker, like a knight in blue and white armour, to take control of the club. He'd seen enough.

The story goes that he was in the car on the way back from some dismal game or other and decided it was time to do something with his money. Jack was from Blackburn and had made his fortune from the steel stockholding business he ran with his brother Fred. When Walkersteel was sold it raised more than £300m and was the biggest private sale in British industrial history. He invested in property, an airline and in Blackburn Rovers. The big money was still some way off, but a flash of Jack's cheque book brought in Bobby Mimms from Spurs for £250,000, which was a club record. Bobby was an honest lad who tried his best and liked a pint but the problem for any goalkeeper was living in the shadow of some of the great keepers we'd had - and he was trying to replace Terry Gennoe, who had been magnificent.

Regardless of the injuries, it was still difficult to see why we were doing so badly. I suppose our collective confidence must have slipped, but I always felt we'd come good sooner or later. It helped that Jack's cash also brought us Steve Livingstone and Tony Dobson from Coventry for £750,000 - it was a sign as to how things were changing.

The money was there, it was obvious to everyone at the club. But those outside wanted a little more reassurance. They didn't realise the scale of Jack's passion and Don's name wasn't strong enough to bring in the players he really wanted. Teddy Sheringham was on the shopping list and turned Don down, but Mike Newell was the classic example. Don tried his best to sign Mike with no luck. As soon as Kenny was in charge, Mike was wearing blue and white. But at least the players he did get helped us to safety. Steve did well, even if he did keep me out of the team for a while, and both Bobby and Tony also played their part. Times were changing, of that there was no doubt, and the impact for the club and for me was about to become clear.

Fitness is a constant worry for footballers. Without it we can't play and ultimately that can mean no job. That's not to say players go out on to the pitch and deliberately avoid physical contact. Far from it - pulling out of a challenge can often do you more harm than going in full-blooded because you put your body into unfamiliar and vulnerable positions when you're trying to keep out of danger. When you go for it in one of

A familiar scene throughout the 1980s.

Me, aged about two, at home in Fishtoft.

On holiday with friends - me holding the ball, of course.

Nanny Garner with my son, John.

Mum and dad in the middle with, on their left, my
brother David's sons, Matthew and Philip, and on
their right, James and John.

With James and John on John's birthday.

A smile while training - see, I did enjoy it!

Five goals in an afternoon against Derby
- not a bad day's work.

Bill Fox congratulates me on my five goals.

"It was never offside!"

In action in the Full Members Cup Final.

Celebrating promotion to the Premier League
- me in the middle.

The view from Blackburn Town Hall
after clinching promotion.

More promotion frolics -
I'm near the back looking cool.

Scoring - the best feeling in the world.

My testimonial game against Newcastle.

With my testimonial committee receiving my cheque.

My debut for West Brom - a "friendly"
against Blackburn Rovers.

Up against Adrian Randall of Burnley
in my West Brom days

A Wembley dream realised -
firing home Wycombe's second goal in the Division
3 Play-off final against Preston in 1994.

Keeping a close eye on the ball as Wycombe take on
Swansea in Division 2 in 1995.

My wedding to Suzy.

With all my boys: James, John and baby Thomas.

those big 50-50 challenges, you're ready for it. I'd been lucky with injuries and the double hernia was the first real problem I'd had. I was getting sharper all the time but it took me until the summer to approach full fitness. Don clearly didn't agree with the progress I'd made and was stalling on my new deal at Ewood. So was I. From my standpoint I was trying to secure improved terms - I felt I'd done my bit to deserve them and I could see the new resources that were coming into the club. Don used the excuse that I wasn't fit and wouldn't agree to a new contract until I'd proved otherwise. We were playing cat and mouse with each other. He clearly felt I might be surplus to requirements if he could land the players he wanted, while I was honest enough to realise that if he didn't get them immediately then he wouldn't be waiting long. It looked like being my last season with the club and with no idea what might be around the corner I was seeking financial security.

Let's be honest, players are much less inclined now to stay with a club for life. With the increase in money comes an increase in mobility and at all levels players - or those still in employment after the ITV Digital disaster - are calling more of the shots than they did even in the mid 1990s when I left the professional game. But loyalty wasn't the only reason I wanted to stay. James and John were happy at school, Mandy and I were getting on well, we had lots of friends in the town and at last it looked like the club was gearing itself up for a big push to promotion. I wanted to be part of that, especially now that, thanks to Jack Walker, the days of counting the tea-bags into the urn were history. Blackburn Rovers had been my employer for fifteen years and I'd drunk some weak tea in my time. Now I fancied a sip of Earl Grey.

Things were changing rapidly. Steve Agnew came in for £750,000 from Barnsley, Stuart Munro arrived from Glasgow

Rangers for £400,000 and on the eve of the new season David Speedie was signed from Liverpool for £400,000. Three things were in my head: these guys were being paid well, the club was readying itself for a proper tilt at promotion and more than at any time during my career my job was well and truly under threat.

On the one hand then, with the new money being injected, I was adamant I deserved better terms and any improvement to my £600 a week would provide increased security for my family. Don was very honest, or he certainly appeared to be, and offered what he said he could. But it was merely an extension on the same terms as before. I took advice from my former teammate Frank Stapleton who was working for Paul Stretford, now one of the major players in the football agency world, and decided to bide my time. As a stop-gap I took the offer of a monthly contract. If another club had come in then at least I'd have a bargaining position to work from. It didn't happen and in true Garner style football came first - I dropped my demands and got on with the job with a contract on exactly the same terms as before. Except my job was changing.

Speedie was clearly the first-choice striker and it was no surprise that I spent much of the early part of the season on the bench. Steve Livingstone and even Lenny Johnrose, who'd come through the youth ranks, were getting the nod over me. Howard Gayle was also still in the squad. The competition up front was strong, though I didn't realise how much tougher it would get as the season progressed.

The spotlight was focussed squarely on Blackburn Rovers. The media was quick to pick up the scent of a club starting to throw cash around and we were one of the bookies' early favourites for the title. The fans, starved of success for so long and witnesses to so many false dawns, were more reticent and the expected big crowds never materialised. Not yet. Their hopes, like those of the players, had been smashed too often before and the cynicism was understandable. It was also well founded because we had a dismal start to the campaign - one point from three league games was bad enough but to cap it all we were dumped out of the Rumbelows' League Cup by Hull City. After the home defeat by Ipswich Town on the last day of August, a game I watched from the bench with fewer than 9,000 supporters for company, Don was given the order of the elbow. It had been coming.

I knew Don well. We'd spent a few years together at the club and had always got on even when I was out of favour, as I clearly was then. Before it was announced he called me into the boardroom and I assumed he was going to explain his thinking behind leaving me out of a losing team, but it was more serious than that.

"The board have asked me to resign, what do you think?"

I might never have had a full grasp of behind-the-scenes politics, but what he should do was obvious.

"I'm not trying to be funny Don, but what's the point in resigning? You've got time left on your contract so if you resign you'll walk away with nothing. If you hang on until they sack you they'll have to pay your contract up."

I reckon he still owes me a pint for that.

He had definitely been under pressure, and while the papers and the supporters were asking questions there was no suggestion he had lost the backing of the playing staff. There's a lot said, too much probably by people who should know better and, if they don't, should keep their thoughts to themselves, about players losing confidence in managers, but I've only seen it happen twice. The first was with Jim Iley at Blackburn and, at the end of my career, with Alan Smith at

Wycombe after he replaced Martin O'Neill. Once you step over the white line you always give 100%, you always want to win. It may not look like that sometimes, but the shirkers are few and far between. At a club like Blackburn where the supporters demanded endeavour, they were almost unheard of. It's a matter of professional and personal pride. But with these characters - Iley and Smith - it was different. You didn't want to lose but if you did it didn't hurt like it should and, at the back of your mind, you're thinking that you want a new manager. It wasn't like that with Don.

He was generally well-liked by the players and that probably had something to do with the fact he was such a soft touch. Don couldn't bollock the players, it just wasn't his style to stand up and give you a good shouting. Even if we were losing games he wouldn't tell us off but, at the same time, he wasn't that constructive either. Whether or not managers shout and scream, they'll eventually work out that they need to talk and work on the training pitch when things are going wrong. We didn't get that with Don, he just didn't seem to have the nous to change our approach or tactics and I think that was part of his undoing. After three promotional near-misses we were nearly relegated, due in part to the fact the opposition knew what we were going to do next.

Before the bigger signings came in we got away with a lot under Don. We used to go on pre-season tours to Sweden with him and on the last trip in 1989 we had to play six games in fourteen days. In previous years we'd stayed in apartments in the middle of nowhere but this time we were given the luxury of a grand hotel and a group of us took full advantage of the facilities and those of the rest of the town by being out every night until two, three, four o'clock in the morning - even if we had a game the next day. It was a good trip because there was a really good bunch around, people like Andy Kennedy, Ally Dawson and Scott Sellars, who could all hold their own in the drinking stakes. Don seemed to have no idea what we were up to until the day before the final fixture. The weather was terrific and we were taking a breather during training in the sunshine. Don sat us all down for what we thought was going to be a routine tactics talk.

"I've just found out what you lot have been up to and it's a disgrace. You're here representing Blackburn Rovers, we've a new season around the corner and you lot are pissing training up a wall."

It was about as strong as he ever got and he couldn't even bring himself to raise his voice. It was like being at school with a soppy teacher who never checked your homework. Then he rounded on Scott. He droned on and on about Scott being a pivotal member of the side, someone who could turn games for us, someone who he would be relying on in the coming season.

"You've got one chance to prove yourself, Scott, and that's tomorrow. Back to work."

The others got up to go and I was just catching up when he pushed me over and jumped on me - literally. I was on the floor with the manager sitting on me. He spoke quietly.

"Simon, I'm excluding you from that discussion."

"What do you mean?"

"Look, you've scored eight goals already on this tour and you can do it - you can go out, drink what you want and still play a good game, but them . . ."

I was flattered.

Scott and I were sharing a room on the trip and that night - an early night - we joked about what Don had said but despite the ribbing Scott felt he had a point to prove. After about twenty minutes of the game Scott nearly ripped the spleen out of his marker. It was an awful challenge and totally out of character. We watched him troop down the tunnel after the red card was flashed. I giggled. He really did prove his point.

Don made his own problems at Blackburn, though, and not just with the players. From the start he'd been an interfering old woman, trying to take control of the club from top to bottom, even the most mundane things.

"How many tea bags in that pot?"

Seriously, he really did ask that of the tea-lady. And he'd try to tell the groundsman his job too, and whoever else was within earshot. It showed a level of insecurity. Perhaps he was already aware of the investment to come and was trying to confirm his own standing around the club. If he'd just concentrated on managing the team I think we may have had more success but he wanted his fingers in every pie. He lost focus towards the end because while the tea tasted great and the pitch was perfect, we were playing crap.

10

REVOLUTIONISING
1991 to 1992

TONY PARKES WAS AGAIN employed to steady the ship in preparation for the new boss. This time I felt it was trickier working under Tony because even he wasn't picking me. That might sound odd but because I had so much respect for him - and he was a pal - I didn't feel it was appropriate me going into his office and demanding to play even though I was performing well in the reserves and in training. It was a tough enough assignment for him as it was and it didn't help that the fans were chanting my name while I was on the bench. That really put him in a quandary - if he was to bring me on was it simply for me to snatch a goal or was it to get the fans off the players' backs? I kept a low profile and did what I could to help the team. My patience paid off because I came back in late September without anyone losing face.

I got my first goal of the season - and it felt like a hell of a wait - away at Millwall early in October. The abuse we received for winning 3-1 at the Den was horrendous but after going four games without a win, I'd have been happy taking three points from the lions at The Colosseum.

It was a good time to start finding the net because by the following Saturday Kenny Dalglish had arrived. I had no inkling Kenny was coming at all, though there was some speculation in the press. Peter White of The Lancashire Evening Telegraph stuck his neck out on Kenny being tempted in and that should have given the game away - Peter tended to be cautious and avoided speculation - but the players didn't have a clue and we weren't told until a couple of days before we played Plymouth in mid-October, and we didn't actually meet him until the day of the game.

Tony picked the team, I think that's the way Kenny wanted to do it and, besides, under Tony we'd lifted ourselves from the bottom of the table to a more stable fifteenth position. I also guessed - wrongly as it turns out - that Kenny didn't really know that much about the players.

He came into the dressing room with Ray Harford an hour before kick-off and introduced himself. We all shook hands - it was a brilliant moment, an unforgettable experience. Here he was, one of my heroes, the player I'd tried to model my game on and now we were going to be on the same side. I was like a schoolkid - totally gobsmacked. I'd played against him a few times in cup matches and just to be on the same pitch as him was a thrill. I used to turn off in those games and watch him work the ball and think bloody hell, what a wonderful player. In fact, I like to think my game was quite like his. Neither of us were out-and-out strikers, though we both scored our fair share, and I was as happy making 'em as banging 'em in. Just like Kenny. If it hadn't been for the accent, no-one would have been able to tell us apart. Much!

Those first few minutes of meeting Kenny and Ray had a lasting impact. Kenny can make an impression just by walking into a room because of who he is and what he's achieved. As for Ray Harford, to be honest I'd never even heard of him. He knew me though, and knew a lot about how I played. That level of homework was impressive.

All the players were on a high. The money was there, that was apparent, now it looked like we'd signed the manager who'd be able to make best use of it and give the club what it had been chasing for so long. I definitely raised my game; I wanted to be picked for the next one. I scored two goals in the Blackburn End and we won the game 5-2. Great, I thought, that should see me picked next week. But I wasn't, I was on the bench. And we lost away at Swindon. I learned a lesson - never assume anything with Kenny Dalglish.

I made a few calls within the game to discover more about Ray and all I kept hearing was about the quality of his coaching. Within a couple of days it was obvious the reputation was deserved - he was first-class. He really knew what he was doing. Training was varied so no-one was ever left on the sidelines twiddling their thumbs, and he kept the players interested - which isn't always that easy. What really gave him the edge over others I've worked with was his ability to explain what he was trying to achieve. With some managers and coaches you can stand around in the freezing rain for twenty minutes while a point is discussed. And still be none the wiser. With Ray, he'd talk for two minutes and the concept became crystal clear, then he'd move on to something else.

At the time we were doing most of our training on the public playing fields at Pleasington, which is on the road to Blackburn crematorium - hardly what Kenny and Ray were used to - and the pitches were terrible which, considering they'd been hammered by God knows how many pub teams over the weekend, was hardly surprising. They must have known what they'd be working with before they arrived and I guess they'd have also known about the club's plans to develop new facilities in the Ribble Valley a few miles out of town, but I doubt if they'd realised the first job each day was to clear away the dog shit.

THERE'S ONLY ONE SIMON GARNER

The early changes to the club were probably more noticeable on the training ground than they were during the games. The players definitely started to give an ounce more effort and the crowds suddenly started to flock down to watch us training. Previously it'd be one man and his dog, a shitting dog at that. Now even the odd cortege would stop for a look on the way back from seeing off their dearly departed. Buddha would have seen the funny side - say a final farewell to one loved one and watch the rebirth of another in the space of an hour.

This sudden upsurge in interest had nothing to do with me or my team-mates, or even what we were doing on a Saturday afternoon; fans just wanted to watch Kenny Dalglish playing five-a-side. That in itself was a boost for the players. Kenny set standards during his career that all footballers should aspire to and training was given a new spirit - it became very competitive. Who wouldn't want to impress the new boss?

One of the weirdest ideas he had - at least it seemed weird at first - was to stop us wearing tracksuit bottoms. He even instructed that we had the pockets in our shorts sewn up. The thinking was that you can't play a match in tracksuit bottoms and there ain't no pockets in match shorts. The more cynical members of the squad reckoned it was to just keep us moving, a fitness-by-necessity regime, because when the wind's up at Pleasington you may as well be north of the Arctic Circle. I've not trained in tracksuit bottoms since. Good habits die hard.

The new management team certainly suited me. I was pretty much a regular first-team choice until Christmas, though that had as much to do with Speedie's suspensions and injuries as anything else. I'd started to bang the goals in and it was particularly gratifying that I was doing this for a new manager who clearly had cash at his disposal. I'd been itching to get off the bench while we were struggling to get goals and now, for a while at least, I was given the opportunity to do just that.

Within a few weeks we were closing in on the teams at the top after sorting out a lot of our problems in training. Ray had got through to us the patterns of play and we started to get that little bit better in terms of organisation. The training procedure was that Tony would usually take the warm-up before Ray took the bulk of the session - he was definitely in charge - with Kenny standing on the sidelines. He'd only really join in for the five-a-side at the end. Ray was coach, he took training; Kenny was manager, he picked the team.

As an example, we were due to play away at Charlton in mid-November, which was a big test for us because as it turned out we sneaked into the play-offs just ahead of them at the end of the season. Ray told us on the Friday that as a one-off we were going to play in the style of Wimbledon, where Ray had worked before, with a long-ball pressing game. We were working on the tactics and Ray sent three players, including midfielder Lee Richardson, to train with the reserves leaving just eleven of us which we assumed was the starting line-up. Almost the minute we arrived at Upton Park, where Charlton were playing at the time, Nicky Reid stripped off and put on his jockstrap, shorts and number four shirt and started going through his stretching routine. Kenny walked into the dressing room at about two o'clock and looked straight at Nicky.

"What are you doing, Nicky?"

"I'm warming up."

"Oh, so you're playing are you?"

Silence.

"Bobby, Keith, Alan, Lee, Colin, Kevin, Jason, Mark, David, Simon, Scott. Craig, you're on the bench with Nicky."

THERE'S ONLY ONE SIMON GARNER

He picked Lee, who'd trained with the reserves the day before and had no idea what we'd been doing while working on this new style of play. We won 2-0. Kenny wasn't trying to prove a point, it was just the way he worked. Just about every other manager I've played under would name his team on the Friday but Kenny would pick a squad of about sixteen - this was in the days when you only had two substitutes - and not announce his selection until an hour before kick-off. I can't say exactly why he did it this way but we reckoned part of it was that you couldn't fall out with the manager at two o'clock on a Saturday if you weren't picked. As soon as the team was named Kenny would slope into the background while Ray talked us through the set-pieces and the tactics. Jack Walker had started to sit in on team-talks too by this point. He was like a dutiful child sitting quietly in the corner, hanging on every word. Despite the millions, despite all his success, I genuinely believe he'd have swapped the lot for a single game in a blue and white shirt.

I was under no illusion about my situation at Blackburn that season. The money was available and now we had a manager who was going to be able to attract the top talent. Kenny had already signed Alan Wright from Blackpool to play at left-back and Colin Hendry had just returned from Manchester City.

There was a rumour going through the dressing-room while Don was still in charge that Colin might be coming back and that some kind of deal had been struck, but nothing happened until Kenny came - surprise, surprise. It was good to have him back and his game had improved massively. Defensively Colin had learnt a great deal and under Kenny and Ray he went from being a very good player to a genuine great.

REVOLUTIONISING

But I was more concerned with the strikers. We already had depth in my position but it was only a matter of time before Kenny started to look at bolstering the forward line. Mike Newell, who had worked under Ray at Luton, was signed in the week following the Charlton match for £1.1m from Everton. It was the club's first ever seven-figure signing and while the figure didn't make any particular impression on me I thought, hang on a minute, now we've got Newell, Speedie, Livingstone, Johnrose and Gayle. And me. I knew I was being pushed down the pecking order.

If I'd thought it before, I knew it now - I was only going to get the odd game from this point on. But I wasn't about to knock on Kenny's door and wave a transfer request in his face. I'd been at Blackburn since 1976 and now, finally, it looked like we might achieve what we'd threatened for so many of those years - and I wanted to be a part of it, I wanted to be there when it happened.

Kenny was very astute with his signings during that period. He came to understand the culture of the club very quickly and I think he was impressed from the start by the atmosphere. It was probably one of the reasons he came to Blackburn after the pressures he'd faced at Liverpool. It had always been a friendly place with a real family atmosphere. Everyone knew each other well and whether you were a player, in the management team, or working behind the scenes, people got on. Mike - and most of the others - fitted into that spirit; he was a great fella, great to be around.

Gordon Cowans arrived around the same time from Aston Villa and he added a whole new dimension to our style of play. If he wasn't the final piece in the jigsaw, he was the one that linked most of the others. He'd played for Villa and Bari and was an England international. His reputation was massive. Baresi would call him from Italy after a game to see how he'd got on - now that's impressive. On the pitch his passing and vision were the best I'd ever seen in a Blackburn shirt but there was more to him than that. He was constructive in training and after games he could dissect the way the match had gone with real clarity. He had it all - thoughtful, intelligent, great player, fine reader of the game. And a great bloke who loved a drink.

Newell's arrival might have been a boon for the team but for me it meant I was back on the bench for the next match against Barnsley, which we won 3-0, and was dropped completely for the first time in the season for the 0-0 draw at Newcastle. Speedie was out for the next three games, he was having a bad time with injuries and suspensions, and so I partnered Mike and we went to the top of the table. Then Speedie was back and I was out of the thirteen that lost at Ipswich, who went on to win the league.

Mike was great to play with. He worked very hard and did a lot of running off the ball, which opened spaces for me and the midfielders to get into, and he never stopped talking - a great team player. Off the pitch he was unassuming, quiet even. He'd turn up and train, have a laugh with the players - he had a wicked dry sense of humour - and got on with everybody.

Speedie, on the other hand, was incredibly selfish and temperamental as a player. That said, he would take weight off partners because defenders would concentrate so much on him that it wasn't unusual for two defenders to sit on him throughout a game. He was also a great header of the ball and a fantastic goalscorer even if he didn't contribute much to the team as a whole.

REVOLUTIONISING

In training he was fiery and obnoxious and never minced his words. He'd tell anybody - including Kenny - if he felt something wasn't right. And he didn't mix that well with the other players. Socially he could be a nightmare. There was always a dark side lurking and once he'd had a few drinks it came out as angry, pathetic nonsense and he'd start picking fights with anybody.

I was glad that Mike was involved in my last goal for Blackburn Rovers. He crossed the ball and I slid in to score in front of our fans at Oxford in a game we won 3-1. By now, every game I played in was a bonus for me. Even if I'd gone out and scored a hat-trick I knew there'd be no guarantee of getting picked for the next match. Under previous managers it would be expected, under Dalglish it was very different and he wanted to use Speedie and Newell together when they were both available. I'd like to say that was a memorable event, my last and 168th league goal for Blackburn, number 192 in total, but it wasn't. After all, I wasn't to know there wouldn't be another. It's a club record and one I doubt will be broken in my lifetime, which is something I'm very proud of.

That was December 7 and we were in the top three. The next day Bill Fox died, which cast a shadow over the whole club. Bill had been chairman since 1982 and had steered the club through the hard times. He was never the most popular figure with the fans because he was forthright and outspoken. And as chairman the supporters would turn on him if things were going badly. But you only have to look at the rest of the clubs in the county to see what he achieved - none of the others enjoyed the kind of stability we had - Burnley, bless 'em, were within a game of joining the Conference and Preston had to apply for re-election to the league. Even Bolton dropped to the Fourth Division.

THERE'S ONLY ONE SIMON GARNER

Bill was a fruit and vegetable merchant and used to have a number of potato suppliers in Boston. He knew my home town well and that created common ground between us. He built the base for Jack Walker to develop and I regret enormously that he never saw the crowning achievement of promotion and, after I'd left, winning the Championship. He was Blackburn Rovers through and through and I was devastated when he died. My dad used to go to most of our away games and Bill would personally ensure he had a ticket.

They say bad news comes in threes. While football's only a game, it was my game, and I was soon on the extreme fringes of the team. That's two. The third was at the shop. I'd never really had any hobbies since my snooker-playing days before I got married. I liked a drink, of course, but it was very much family and football. But I did move into the fashion trade for a while.

Rococco was supposed to be my pension fund. I worked there every day after training - it was midway between home and Pleasington, about two minutes from each. As a sideline to my real job of kicking a lump of leather round the park it was OK but as time passed it was obvious it wasn't going to provide for my family just on its own. But I had partners and felt responsible for the business.

My investment was £7,000, which came from my testimonial fund, and my partners were Andy McKie and Ian Battersby. We'd socialised as families and were pretty close and I think it was one drunken night that we decided to go for it. Well, you're only young once.

Initially we'd considered a sports shop but we felt for that to succeed we'd have to go into the town centre where the rent and rates were out of our reach. There was also a lot of competition but there weren't many quality clothes shops.

REVOLUTIONISING

I knew I was hardly in George Best's league - and even his shops folded - but I had a good team and I wanted something to fall back on. So we bought a shop on Preston Old Road at Cherry Tree and opened Rococco by Simon Garner.

My name was attached to the signage purely for marketing purposes, to try and get people in knowing there was a good chance I'd be about. And business, to begin with, was brisk. Obviously you have your ups and downs but I was getting good advice from my mum who had been a partner in a high class ladieswear shop back home.

"Be patient, Simon. It'll take you three years to get that business going."

And she was right. We weren't making any real money, but we weren't losing either, which was the main thing.

Ian's wife Sue and Mandy put most of the hours in. Yvonne, Andy's wife, rented some space at the back of the shop for ladies' clothes while Mandy and Sue dealt with the men's. I enjoyed the work and it was the closest I'd ever come to having a proper job. Some punters would come in just to talk to me about football without the slightest intention of buying anything, but that was fine - I've always been happy to talk football with fans. I did have one or two problems from Burnley fans though. There was an infamous incident when some of the 100 Club crew clubbed together to send a plane over Turf Moor after another disappointing season with a banner flying from the tail. The message read, "Staying down forever. Love Rovers. Ha ha ha." Now don't get me wrong, that was very, very funny. But, contrary to popular belief, I had nothing to do with it and I didn't even know it had been planned. One of the first things Blackburn fans ever ask me is about the aeroplane and none of them ever believe it wasn't my work. I even said so in the

Lancashire Evening Telegraph at the time but it made no difference.

Anyway, back to the shop. I think it was some time after the plane incident that we got a call saying a Burnley fan had been in and left a bomb. Well ho-bloody-ho. I can only assume the call came from the same headcases at Burnley who, rumour had it, had devised a method of bringing down the roof at the Blackburn End terrace by removing a single brick, because I knew for a fact there was no bomb in the shop.

I'd been behind the counter since we'd opened and we hadn't had a single customer in the shop. And while that's nothing to be proud of, it meant the stock was safe for another day.

After the ram-raid it was a different story and it was difficult to raise a smile then.

I was at home in the evening and got a call from the police saying the shop had been ransacked. The stock had been completely stripped out. The fella who owned the sweet shop next door told me four or five lads in balaclavas pulled up in a car, rammed through the shutters, nicked the stuff and sped off. It wasn't the first time the shop had been turned over, but ram-raiding seemed a bit excessive. There was nothing I could do other than board up the windows and get back to Mandy and the kids.

The next morning I got another call from the police saying the car had been found about a mile from the shop, and I later learned that the car belonged to Gordon Cowans. It'd been taken from outside the Trafalgar Hotel, near Preston, where he was staying.

"Alright Gordon, found your car yet?"

"How do you know it's gone?"

"Because you drove it through my shop window last night you thieving bastard!"

REVOLUTIONISING

"I don't suppose my golf clubs are still there?"

It became even less amusing when it came to convincing the insurance company that it wasn't an inside job. We closed the shop shortly afterwards. After four serious thefts and dwindling profits you start to question why you're bothering.

Meanwhile, all was well at Ewood Park even if I was only getting the occasional appearance as a substitute. We were top but for the first time we were starting to feel the pressure. The expectation was getting higher by the week and the fans thought we were going to walk to the new Premier League. But it doesn't happen like that and we were brought back down to earth when Notts County knocked us out of the FA Cup. That shocked us because we'd become so used to winning and it knocked some reality into us. Thankfully we regained our form in the league and had a three-match winning run culminating in a 3-1 victory over Newcastle. Speedie scored a great hat-trick that day, but the main talking point was the fact that Mike Newell broke his leg.

That opened the door for me again, particularly as Speedie was missing for the next three games as well, but the loss of Mike was a terrible blow. People remember Speedie as being the main man that season because he scored twenty-four and made the headlines, but Mike's role shouldn't be overlooked. After the Newcastle game we only got fourteen more points from the next seventeen games and eight of those came from the last four matches - when Mike was back in the starting line-up. Mike made the difference when it mattered.

I was definitely out of favour now. I played three games in which we only picked up two points but only had a recognised striker to partner me in one of them. Inevitably the chequebook was out again. Chris Price was now back at the club having re-signed from Villa for £100,000. Bob Saxton originally brought Chris from Hereford for £25,000 not long before he was sacked and he proved an excellent buy, which wasn't lost on Aston Villa, who paid £125,000 for him two years later. I don't think we ever satisfactorily replaced Chris who could happily operate at right-back or right-midfield and he was just the kind of player to bolster the squad at a tricky time. I was surprised when he came back though, because he left under something of a cloud. I don't know the full story, but there was definitely some bad blood there. There was a feeling he may get a rough ride from the fans but they took to him again straight away - scoring a goal in each of his first two games back might have helped.

Tim Sherwood also joined and was an unknown quantity to everyone having come from Watford via Norwich. Kenny paid £500,000 for him and in his first season, when he barely got a game, it didn't look the best buy in the world; three years later as club captain and with the Premier League trophy in his hands, it was a different story. Oh, and another striker was introduced - Roy Wegerle from QPR, another £1.1m man.

This was an unusual signing and didn't seem to fit Kenny's other buys. Roy was a very skilful player, a magician with the ball, but he gave the impression that he'd rather be anywhere other than in an English climate.

"It's cold. I'd rather be surfing."

And he meant it. Not surprisingly, he ended his career in America. The problem was that Roy was an individualist and we needed team players who would graft to get us out of the division. We were never a flair side and if you think about the teams Kenny played in and managed it was always the case that the whole was more important than the component parts. Still, I was the guy who favoured Hill over May and Skinner over Wilcox, so what did I know?

REVOLUTIONISING

March was a tough month for the team and for me. I'd completely dropped out of the starting thirteen and we were struggling. The tabloid vultures were out and after a 3-0 win at Brighton we managed to lose six on the trot. My final appearance in a Blackburn shirt was in the first of that sequence, I came on as a substitute as Charlton beat us 2-0 at home. The bookies had long since stopped taking bets on us to win the Second Division title and they'd have stood to lose a fortune if we'd kept our mid-season form together. Bookies, though, tend to be rich people and we eventually helped them add to their pile.

The club remained calm and Kenny and Ray carried on as if it was a mild cold, not the full-blown pneumonia everyone else - particularly the very twitchy fans - considered it to be. The supporters, like me, had seen it all before - great promise and then bugger all to show for it. Given I was fit at this point and that we'd only lost one league game all season when I'd been on from the kick-off, I thought I might be due a recall. Speedie was off the boil, Wegerle was struggling to get goals and fit in with the style of play and Newell was still being treated for his injury. But no - Kenny went and paid Swindon Town, who were still in with a shout of the play-offs, £700,000 for their top-scorer Duncan Shearer just before the transfer deadline.

Duncan had built a reputation for being a big, powerful lad who scored a lot of goals, which was exactly what we needed at the time, though I felt Kenny could have done a lot worse than to take a chance on me instead. Luck was at a premium for us then and even Duncan, who'd scored thirty for Swindon, couldn't make a difference. I saw his debut at Barnsley - I'd gone with some mates and sat in the stand - where he scored his only goal for Blackburn. We still lost. The next game, midweek at Port Vale, was even worse. They were bottom of the league and gave us a 2-0 hiding.

It's at times like these you just need to get away and get your head together. Or in Kenny's case grab a bag of golf clubs and hitch a ride out of town. He took us to his homeland for a breather and we had a ten-day break before our next game at Watford. It was time to get down to some serious bonding. And golfing. And drinking. The hotel was in Stirling, but I couldn't tell you which golf course it was perched on because I have as much interest in golf as I have in National No Smoking Day. Most of the players played solidly for the two days. I did a bit of swimming.

Events like these tend to fall at a time when there's a few glum faces appearing at a club. Just to get away for a couple of days in a fresh environment can help break any staleness and improve morale, especially when you get a couple of good nights out thrown into the bargain. Invigorated and ready for the challenge ahead - we were still second and in an automatic promotion position - we headed back down the M6. Then we lost to Watford and to Wolves and to Leicester. So much for a refreshing break.

By the end of the losing streak in mid-April when Leicester, one of our promotion rivals, beat us 1-0 at home, the unthinkable had happened - we'd even dropped out of the play-off zone. In just a few months we'd turned from a club who were seen as a quaint, loveable outfit, a club the press and fans from outside the area had a real soft-spot for because of how friendly it was and how close we'd come to having success, to one people wanted to see fail. It was jealousy I suppose. Jealousy at the resources that were being pumped in. That and the fact the media love nothing more than a fallen hero.

REVOLUTIONISING

This wasn't lost on our opponents. While we weren't playing particularly well we had become a prized scalp. Big crowds were watching us wherever we went and opposition players raised their game to take us on. It was only natural. In the big cup games against First Division sides, we always wanted to prove a point too. Now we were on the receiving end. We were the moneybags boys; we were football enemy number one.

Despite everything there were no panic buttons being pressed within the camp. Training didn't change and we didn't alter the game plan. Visibly Kenny didn't seem to be under pressure at all. The dressing-room feeling was still good, we were still up for the challenge and genuinely believed we'd still be promoted even if it was through the backdoor of the play-offs.

It's impossible to put a finger on what was going wrong, it was just one of those things. We'd got to the top very quickly and Kenny and Ray wouldn't let us get complacent, it wasn't in their vocabulary, and our feet were kept firmly on the ground. We started the season badly then had a great run and like all clubs we hit a rocky patch. Only ours didn't seem to stop and it was made worse because we were expected to win every match. They kept us motivated during that run and made sure we didn't lose belief in ourselves. Even though I wasn't playing I still felt it all applied to me. That was an indicator of the qualities of Kenny and Ray - no-one was excluded from the team effort.

We scraped our first point in over a month with a 2-2 draw at Tranmere on Easter Monday, which was Newell's first start since the Newcastle match in February. He scored from the spot but there was still a lot of work to be done. We beat Millwall 2-1 the following Saturday in front of

12,820 fans - our lowest gate since before Christmas - and then we were at home to Sunderland when Scott Sellars brought us level with a great shot near the end. That left one league game left at Plymouth. I wasn't on the trip, but the nerves were still intense for me. It would have been easier being with the squad, being so distant from it was horrendous. We were confident we had the talent to take us up through the play-offs, but we were still sweating on making it over the final hurdle.

Plymouth needed to win to avoid relegation; we needed to win to be sure of being in the play-offs. Speedie came up trumps with a hat-trick. Play-offs again, then. Record so far - played in three, lost in three.

We scraped through the semi-fianl after a backs-against-the-wall performance of real grit at the Baseball Ground, and then it was Wembley. While I knew there was no way I'd ever be playing, or that I'd even be considered for the bench, it was still one of my best days in football.

I'd played my part that season and had been proud of my achievements, despite the limited opportunities. And I've Kenny Dalglish to thank for the memories because he made sure I was among the three non-playing squad members assigned a seat on the bench that day, even though my bum barely touched it all afternoon, and took me down for the whole trip rather than have me just turn up on the day. While I felt I deserved to be part of what turned out to be such a historic day, I was no less grateful to Kenny for making it happen.

Even in the best circumstances it was going to be a difficult game to watch. I'd been to Wembley before, of course, for the Full Members Cup Final, but this was such a one-off game, such a massive game, that my experience didn't count for much and there was little I could offer my team-mates in terms of how to prepare for the experience.

Wembley that day was baking hot. Tony Parkes was asked to lead the team out. That was another great touch by Kenny. Tony had been at the club since 1970 and this was the biggest day for Blackburn for any of us. He had contributed so much in so many ways and he deserved this moment in the spotlight.

You hear players talking about playing in the shadow of the Twin Towers, and they talk about how little they remember of the game. It was the same for me that day, just as it had been for the Full Members Cup. No matter how hard you try, the occasion gets the better of you.

We didn't play particularly well - I remember that much - and there wasn't much between the teams in the first half and precious few chances. Then, just before half-time, Speedie was decked by Steve Walsh in the box.

The referee was George Courtney in his last senior game. Courtney, not that anyone really needs reminding of it, was the guy who gave Palace the so-called penalty which meant we missed promotion in 1989 and since then the fans had given him terrible stick every time he was involved in our games. As Speedie went down, it was like slow-motion, and it felt an age until Courtney awarded the penalty. Newell held his nerve and sent Carl Muggleton the wrong way. It was mayhem on the pitch, the bench and in the crowd.

After the break, the game livened up but Leicester were in control and we cleared the ball off the line more than once. Kevin Moran and Colin Hendry performed heroics. We even got another penalty which Mike struck well, but Muggleton made the right choice this time and stopped it.

THERE'S ONLY ONE SIMON GARNER

If my description of this game, the most important in my sixteen years at Blackburn, is sketchy, that's for two reasons. Firstly, as I mentioned, the occasion gets the better of you. Secondly, I didn't actually watch much of the second half, I was too busy smoking myself to an early grave.

It would be wrong to say I was nervous, I wasn't. Shuddering wreck would be a more appropriate description. And thank god for the portaloo. There, half-way up the tunnel, my very own smoker's corner. I don't know if it was there for the Queen's private use or something but I was in there every ten minutes having a fag because I was so nervous.

We won, we were up. And so was my time at Blackburn.

The celebrations were, of course, incredible. On the pitch and off it. The journey home was a blur, though I still have a memory fixed in my brain of seeing Kenny swigging from a champagne bottle on the coach and waving to fans as we headed up the motorway.

And I'll certainly never forget seeing him force that ample rear through a window at the Woodlands pub on Preston New Road because, quite simply, we couldn't get in the front door!

The reception we were given at the Town Hall was another brilliant occasion, though one tinged with a touch of poignancy for me. The crowd launched into a lengthy refrain of 'There's Only One Simon Garner' and, drunk on a combination of beer and emotion, I conducted it from the balcony.

I knew it was the last time I'd hear it as an employee of Blackburn Rovers and I milked it for all it was worth.

11

LEAVING
1992 to 1994

ONCE AGAIN, I HAD KENNY to thank - this time for ensuring I remained a first team footballer. Ossie Ardiles, a good friend from his brief time at Ewood Park, was keen to sign me but couldn't stump up the £100,000 demanded by the Blackburn board.

I really wanted a free transfer and felt, after all the loyalty I'd shown the club, I deserved it. I spoke with Ossie about it.

"Simon, the most we can afford is £30,000. If they let you go on a free, the money's yours. If they want £20,000, you can have the difference."

I knew I had to speak to Kenny or I was stuck playing in the reserves.

"Ossie can't afford more than £30,000, boss, which is a long way short of what the board wants."

"Sorry Simon, can you just move to your left a bit."

Typical Kenny. He wanted to see an important putt in some golf tournament or other and I was blocking his view of the telly.

"Now then, what was that?"

I explained the situation and asked if he could help.

"Leave it with me."

Kenny knew how important it was for me, now in my thirties, to be playing. He was honest enough to say I'd be a fringe player and the best I could really hope for was a few starts on the bench. All of which I already knew because it was clear he was aiming for a big signing and that eventually turned out to be Alan Shearer. There are worse players to lose your place to!

Kenny was true to his word and delivered a compromise that kept the board reasonably happy and, while I didn't make a bean on the deal, at least I had what I really wanted - a starting position in a decent club. The fee was £30,000 and I packed my bags.

It was an odd sensation. There are plenty of players who have moved clubs six or more times in a career but for me it was something I don't think I was prepared for. I was moving away from home to live in Birmingham and I was going to have to get used to a new lifestyle, a new club and a lot of new names. It was like being a teenager again. In all respects.

At least I knew Ossie and didn't think I needed to prove myself to him, but that still left the players, officials, fans and media. My first duty was to try and match the most expensive player in history with, incredibly, a friendly against Blackburn Rovers. I think it was Shearer's debut for Blackburn and all eyes were on him. The crowd was small but the Rovers fans gave me a great reception. I scored first then Shearer grabbed two. Show-off. Still, it must have been funny for those who saw me following the Blackburn players towards the away dressing-room before being reminded I was heading the wrong way.

I settled in quickly. There was a good team spirit and some serious drinkers to keep up with. The original deal was I'd train in Blackburn for the first part of the week, then travel to the Midlands on the Thursday and stay until the Saturday game before heading back home again. On paper that seemed fairly reasonable. I'd only be away from home for a couple of nights a week and that suited Mandy. Except we were playing a lot of midweek games and that meant I'd end up away for the best part of a week. The cracks in our relationship started to emerge at that point. I didn't help matters either. I could be in a hotel room for five nights a week or I'd stay over at our goalkeeper Stuart Naylor's place, an arrangement that became more or less permanent after a while, and we'd do a lot of drinking. It was a new lease of life for me and though I know it was selfish and I missed the boys, I couldn't get enough of it.

Ossie's training was brilliant and in complete contrast to the way I'd worked before - and I'd been through a few coaches and managers. Ossie's was a simple approach - play football all day. The way that converted on to the pitch was in an all-out attacking style. There was no doubt I'd lost a bit of pace since the hernia operation so that suited me down to the ground because I wasn't expected to do much tracking back, just concentrate on getting forward. Pass, pass, pass was Ossie's motto. Keith Burkinshaw was there as his coach and he'd work out set-piece routines but Ossie wouldn't let it drag on, he didn't want the players to be bored.

That season we were top scorers in the league though unsurprisingly our defensive record wasn't great. We were pushing for promotion and the supporters loved the way we were playing - if we conceded a goal it didn't matter because we had the confidence to get another ourselves. The fans were fantastic - crowds were regularly over 16,000 at home and 4,000 would be at the away games. And this was in Division Two.

I was doing well, too. Until I picked up another serious injury. We were playing at Swansea and I just collapsed in a nothing challenge. I was given an x-ray and told that it would settle under physiotherapy. I had massage treatment all week and was selected to play against West Ham in a cup match. I hit a left-footed volley and went down in agony. The hospital said I'd broken two bones in my ankle and leg and I was out for six weeks.

But what a way to come back. It was against Burnley and I needed one more goal to hit my career two-hundred-mark. The chairman had words with me on the day before the game.

"If you score and it's in front of the Burnley fans, you are not allowed to celebrate."

With two minutes on the clock and with my first touch of the game I scored right in front of their fans. A temporary bout of amnesia meant I was back in the chairman's office on the Monday. It's another of those incidents that seems to have found its way into Blackburn folklore and people still ask me about taking my West Brom shirt off to reveal a Blackburn shirt underneath. Yes I made a meal of the goal in front of their fans but I have to confess the two-shirts story has absolutely no truth in it whatsoever. It's just a pity I hadn't thought of it before kick-off.

I struggled to get a regular place in the side though, partly because I was picking up niggling injuries and also because Ossie signed Andy Hunt, who was a great goalscorer, and so I spent some time on the bench watching him and Bob Taylor. Bob was adored at West Brom. In a lot of ways he kept the pressure off me because he was a hero. It was nice to walk into the club realising there was someone else to shoulder the burden of goalscoring expectation. But I knew I'd have to work hard to convince the fans of my own value because I'd seen the treatment given to new strikers by Blackburn fans.

We finished the season fourth and went into the play-offs. We beat Swansea in the semi-final and met Port Vale at Wembley. I was on the bench again, but not in a suit this time.

LEAVING

While we won the game I still feel the play-offs are wrong, regardless of the fact it spins the season out for more clubs. This was my fifth play-offs and in none of those cases had my team finished in the top three, which should be the real dividing line between success and failure. Still, it was a fantastic drinking session when we won. We cruised the game 3-0 and I came on for a few minutes at the end. Nicky Reid, who was at West Brom too, scored that day and it was deafening - out of the 52,000 at the game there were 40,000 from the Midlands.

We had an open-top bus trip round West Bromwich and Birmingham and the bottles never dried up. For two or three days we just didn't stop drinking. And that's just about my last happy memory of West Brom.

Ossie left for Tottenham, a dream job for him, and Keith Burkinshaw was appointed manager, a nightmare for me. I'd never really seen eye-to-eye with Keith. The first time we crossed swords, while Ossie was still around, was when I said I didn't go on to the pitch to warm-up until the teams were led out by the referee. He called me a lazy bastard.

"Yes, he is a lazy bastard, Keith, but this lazy bastard will score goals."

Keith didn't like Ossie undermining him. I spent most of the time in Division One on the bench and in the reserves. That meant I was rarely home for more than a day or two each week because the reserves played midweek and I was on call each weekend too. The strain was starting to show on the marriage. Mandy and I weren't communicating through anything much more than strained small-talk about the kids and there were too many arguments for sanity's sake. And I was still enjoying my bachelor lifestyle. While I wasn't chasing women, I was drinking plenty and generally re-living my childhood. Mandy wasn't impressed and neither was Keith. He didn't like his players drinking, a sentiment not shared by many in the dressing-room.

The core drinking squad was me, Gary Robson, Stuart Naylor and Darren Bradley. Keith would come into training and slyly try to smell our breath for booze. Stuart and I got wise to it and invested in extra strong mints and aftershave but Keith was quite happy to send Gary home if he got a whiff. The writing was clearly on the wall for me and it came to a head on a trip to Halifax, strangely, for a cup match. We took a squad of seventeen and I didn't even get on the bench. They were a non-league team and beat us 2-1. The next day we were off to Italy to play an Anglo-Italian game and get a bit of a break in what was proving a tricky season. When we got back to Birmingham from Halifax, Keith turned to me and told me, without offering a reason, that I wasn't on the trip. That was harsh and I eventually submitted a transfer request.

It dragged on and on and it was embarrassing because no-one was interested in me. Then I heard that Wycombe Wanderers had made an enquiry. And then it dragged on some more. Everything was settled at West Brom, they were letting me go on a free transfer, but it still took ten weeks for the deal to go through. It was a nightmare. I could never get past Martin O'Neill's secretary to speak to him and Keith wouldn't even talk to me in the corridors at West Brom. I couldn't work him out because I don't think I'd been disruptive at all. Bloody hell, David Speedie had come on loan during Ossie's time - now that was disruptive. He was dropped for one game and we never saw him again.

Finally the move happened and everyone was happy. Everyone, that is, except Mandy. She was happy for me to get a transfer but wanted me to go back to the north. Not only had I just signed for Wycombe, another hundred miles down the motorway, I didn't want to go back home.

It was depressing that they were the only club to come in for me, because I still felt I had a lot to offer. And this was a drop of two divisions into the basement of the football league. It wasn't how I'd have planned the end of my career. But it kept me in a living and my wages stayed the same.

When I realised how desperate I was to go, I knew the marriage really was over. I tried to persuade myself it was for the best, particularly for the boys. I didn't want them living in a home when I was resentful of having to be there and because I had no choice about where I next worked. I didn't want them uprooting from school. But in reality it was much simpler and much more self-motivated - despite missing the kids, I loved being on my own. The boys were devastated when I told them, even though they knew things weren't right between me and their mum. The worst thing was the distance. I spoke to them every night but it's just not the same as being there.

12

WANDERING
1994 to 1996

I DON'T THINK MARTIN felt he was taking a gamble when he signed me. He'd watched me enough and had sent scouts out to see me.

With Wycombe new to the league I think he felt he needed someone with experience. The club had just sold Keith Scott to Swindon for £300,000 and I was seen as a solid replacement.

I was straight into the first team, which after such a long period of rotting away on the bench and in the reserves was a welcome boost. Now I've played with some interesting striking partners over the years - Speedie, Newell and Stapleton among them - but my experience at Wycombe was something new. Tim Langford was his name and until Wycombe were promoted to the league the season before he'd been a postman! But like the others who packed in their former jobs he was ambitious, determined and a decent player.

It took me three games to find the net, a cup match at Swansea that we lost 2-1. But I was back in business. We were in the top half of the table when I arrived and I was having the time of my life. It was like starting all over again, except this time I was the experienced pro. My age apart, it was like being at Blackburn in the early days. It was a family club with a great manager and the players were a fantastic bunch who lived and breathed football without any sense of ego playing a part.

And when you combine that with the fact that these lads had just realised their life's ambition of being professional football players, some of them at a very late age, then the sense of excitement that was around the place every day was understandable.

The standard of football was much higher than I'd expected too. Martin's philosophy was to play to our strengths and not to worry about our deficiencies - a dream to a player like me. So long as we scored more than the opposition, he didn't care how many we conceded. We rarely practised set-pieces, rather we'd play by instinct. Anyone would take a corner or throw-in and we weren't assigned positions to defend or attack at particular points in the game. Martin was much keener that we use our heads and take responsibility for situations ourselves. It made us an attractive attacking side.

The training facilities weren't ideal, but neither were the ones we used at Blackburn even when Kenny was manager, but the Adams Park Stadium was - and is - a great place to play. They used to have a ground that was renowned in the game for having a nasty slope but Adams Park was purpose-built and has been improved over the years to hold about 10,000.

The proceeds from the old ground had been put to good use - and not just by developing the new stadium. Money was earmarked for Martin to make his players feel good about life in the league and we had a hotel stop-over for almost all our away games. Martin was a god at Wycombe and if he'd asked for gold-plated goalposts I think he would have been given them.

If tactics were never part of his make-up in those days, motivation certainly was. He had an uncanny ability to understand the needs of individuals and slot them into the requirements of the team. He was perfectly happy for us to have a drink in the bar on the night before a game and because he treated the players like grown-ups they didn't abuse his generosity.

I got to know him very well. There isn't that much between us in terms of age - he's only seven years older than me - and I think it was useful for him to be able to speak to someone who'd recently played at a high level with some of the best managers in the game. Alan Parry, the television commentator and a big Wycombe fan, was also someone I got to know well and the three of us and our partners would often share a drink. Alan later helped me get some work as a pundit for Sky Sports.

For the club and for me it was a great season. I was enjoying my game again and Martin's magic was working well. We finished the season fourth, a remarkable achievement, and though I know it sounds big-headed, I made it into Wycombe folklore.

Once again I was in the play-offs and once again I put my prejudices about the end-of-season lottery to one side. Carlisle were our first opponents and I scored in both games to reach the final 4-2 on aggregate. What a feeling. I knew I was coming towards the end of my career, but what a way to do it - back to Wembley again. And back in another team with my old Blackburn room-mate Nicky Reid, who'd now followed me to Wycombe after we'd been together at West Brom.

Our opponents for the final were Preston who, under John Beck, were a nightmare to play against. Beck was at the opposite end of the managerial spectrum to Martin. There was a routine for everything and the style of play made Wimbledon at their worst look pretty. Long balls into the corners, long balls over the midfield, long balls to force throw-ins. It wasn't football as I knew it, but it was bloody effective.

WANDERING

There was some speculation that he'd wanted to sign me before I joined the Wycombe revolution, but there were two reasons I could never have done that. Firstly, I wasn't big enough and, more importantly, I would have hated playing that style of football.

What we did have on our side, though, was the knowledge of exactly how they'd approach the game. We, on the other hand, didn't have routines, so god knows how anyone prepared to play against us.

Everyone was desperate to play their part in what could be the biggest moment in the history of the club. Paul Hyde, our keeper, was in a terrible state. His guts were mangled, he was being sick and had dreadful diarrhoea. He lost half a stone in the days leading up to the final and I'd say he was about 20% fit, but there was no way on earth he was going to miss this game.

Martin's team talk was one of the easiest he's ever given.

"Look, you know how to play them. We know what's coming. Get it on the ground, play football and let the ball do the work. Preston will get knackered."

And they did get knackered.

The first twenty minutes were incredible. The ball fizzed from end to end and we had the opportunities to make the game safe before the break but we went behind - a long throw, surprisingly enough, which led to an overhead kick.

We were level within a minute when I played a neat ball through the channel for Steve Thompson, who had been in the RAF, to score. But that joy was short-lived and we conceded again.

I couldn't believe we were losing at half-time - none of us could. But we stuck to our game-plan and played the only way we knew how. And then it happened.

THERE'S ONLY ONE SIMON GARNER

A looping ball came from Dave Titterton in midfield. I was eight yards out with a defender on my back, I controlled it with my right foot and stuck a beauty away with my left. I'd scored at Wembley. After nearly twenty years in the professional game I'd achieved something I'd only previously dreamed of. Even at the time I understood how important it was to me on a personal level.

Even before we'd equalised a second time, I never felt we could lose the game. We were just too good for them and we had a team with spirit and skill. And so it proved.

Our third was a great move. Steve Guppy, I think it was, played through to Thompson and he put a great ball through the defenders to me. I could have turned and struck but I saw Dave Carroll on the right and he was unmarked. I swivelled and passed into his path for a sweet finish.

I thought he might have returned the favour for our fourth but he beat three defenders, then turned two of them again to get the ball on to his right foot before finishing a brilliant solo goal.

I even had time to 'score' one of the goals of my career from just inside their half. I was given offside. It was the wrong decision.

But what a day, what a season.

Before I joined, the club made the third round of the FA Cup, then went out to Norwich City; in the Coca Cola Cup they beat Coventry at home but lost on aggregate and, in my debut match, we beat Fulham in the Autoglass Trophy southern semi-final. We lost the area final to Swansea, who went on to the grand final at Wembley. But two trips in a season to the Twin Towers would have been greedy!

I was interviewed straight after beating Preston.

"You didn't want to play in the Third Division for very long, did you, Simon?"

WANDERING

He was spot on. No, I didn't, and I was glad to have played a part in getting Wycombe into the second. It was one of the best seasons of my career, even if it only started with my transfer in February.

We went back to the ground and hosted a serious party.

I never imagined life in the Second Division was going to be easy. And it wasn't. But Martin worked more miracles. He signed Cyril Regis and he made me feel very good - not only was he an excellent player, but at thirty-six he was a year older than me!

We were, by some measure, the oldest strikeforce in the league. But while I was in pretty good nick, Cyril was ridiculously fit and, if I'm honest, was more useful to Wycombe that season than I was. But as a partnership we were great.

In many ways what we achieved in the 94-95 season was more remarkable than the promotion campaign. A personal highlight was scoring the first ever goal at Huddersfield's McAlpine Stadium in a game we won 1-0. But much more than that, we almost made it into the play-offs again.

That season there was a restructuring taking place and five clubs were being relegated. I think we all felt we had to keep our noses clean to keep away from that pack, but Martin refused to even consider a season of consolidation. What was the point? He'd always wanted us to play to our abilities, so there was no way we were going to be able to change that now and start trying to close games down. And anyway, our fans were used to real football and that approach would have bored them rigid.

It was a gamble, but one which almost came off. Despite a run of rotten form to rival even the darker days at Blackburn - eight games without a win leading up to Easter - we finished sixth which, in most years, would have seen us into the play-offs. That season it was top five only. One team to be automatically promoted with the next four into the lottery. Huddersfield finished fifth, just three points above us, and were promoted with Birmingham City.

A week after the end of our season, Blackburn Rovers were crowned champions of England. I'd spent the day in Windsor having lunch and an extended drinking session with some friends and only learned the results when I got home late in the evening. I'd like to have celebrated. The only trouble was that I was already pissed and crashed into bed wearing a big smile.

Later in the summer I was asked to summarise for the radio at Wembley for the Charity Shield. I've never been a particular fan of the fixture and this didn't change just because Blackburn Rovers were in it. I cut a deal with the commentator that I'd watch the game in the bar, which was pretty close to the press box, and pop back to the microphone when something interesting happened.

After the game I went to talk with some of my old friends in the bar and saw Jack Walker chatting to Terry Venables. Having had the odd half over the course of the afternoon I had no hesitation in going over to offer my congratulations to Jack on the season.

"Erm, Mr Walker . . ."

I got halfway through the sentence and he immediately broke off from speaking to Venables and we nattered like long-lost buddies. We might not have had much else in common, but we were both Blackburn through and through.

Nobody I knew blamed Martin for leaving Wycombe. He'd served the club admirably. He took them from the semi-pro ranks to the brink of Division One, the highest level I played at. I owe him so much for rescuing my career, for giving me a chance to play the kind of football I'd always wanted to play in an atmosphere that just couldn't be beaten.

As for the other players, you have to remember that two years earlier most of them had proper jobs in the real world. Thanks to Martin and the vision of the club, dreams had come true.

When Martin left for Norwich it was a sad day but one which brought back some of the best memories I'd had in the game.

So why did Alan Smith have to go and fuck it all up?

I'm not just saying that because he didn't fancy me much, though he obviously didn't. The whole place just lost its momentum from the minute he arrived. As managerial appointments go, the only one to rival it in my life in the game was that of Jim Iley at Blackburn.

So before I'm accused of whingeing and whining because he ended my professional career, let's lay a few facts on the line.

Under Martin we finished sixth in Division Two. Under Smith we finished twelfth. He dumped Steve Thompson, Paul Hyde and Terry Howard into non-league football. He changed the first team kit to resemble that of Crystal Palace, where he'd previously worked. He made us train at Bisham Abbey where the facilities were good, expensive and, coincidentally I'm sure, where Smith had his tennis lessons. He presided over the worst attendance in the league history of the club and looked on as the Wycombe board announced record losses of £300,000 for the season.

He was finally dismissed at the start of his second season after the club was humiliated 6-3 by Peterborough after leading 3-1. It took years for the club to recover and while I'm not a bitter person by nature, his treatment of me left an enduring bad taste in my mouth.

THERE'S ONLY ONE SIMON GARNER

He even told me to stop smoking. I mean, bloody hell.

I was out of the first team, though I'm not sure why because I was playing pretty well, and I was in good shape. At the first whiff of loaning me out I was off to Torquay. They obviously wanted me pretty badly because they organised a chauffer-driven car to get me there. I accepted the offer on the condition I wouldn't have to live in Devon. It was just too far from home.

And, in all honesty, that was the problem with Torquay in general and why they're always going to struggle - just about every game involves a million mile round-trip.

Still, I enjoyed myself even though they were a poor side and finished the season at the very bottom of the league. Eddie May was the manager and doing his best in the most difficult circumstances imaginable. Rodney Jack was playing at the time for them and he was a great guy to have in the side because he was fast as lightning. And I wasn't.

The chairman was a good laugh too. Mike Bateson he was called, and he had this great habit of inviting players into the boardroom for a few bevvies after the game. And I also got to know the television presenter Helen Chamberlain pretty well too. She really is a mad Torquay fan and used to drive from London to the game after presenting Soccer AM on Sky Sports.

I played nine matches and got one goal for Torquay, my last in professional football. It was February 3, 1996 and it wasn't a bad strike - a cross from the left which I volleyed home. And that goal won me a bet. Fulham's keeper was Tony Lange, a team-mate from my West Brom days. It was a pint on him if I scored and a pint on me if I didn't. I think buying the pint hurt more for Tony than picking the ball out of the net because he was never known for being first man at the bar.

WANDERING

When I got back to Adams Park I didn't get another game under Smith and I was starting to get a bit concerned for my future. My contract was up at the end of the season and I knew I had no chance of being offered anything else with Smith even though, at thirty-six, I think there was still a job I could do.

But nothing could prepare me for the way I left the full-time ranks.

Over the years lots of people have asked me about moving into the coaching or management side of the game. And my answer has always been the same, that it's not for me. And a lot of it is to do with cowardice. I don't want to be the guy who has to tell kids who have their hearts set on a career in the game that they're not up to scratch, I don't want to be the guy who has to show the door to an experienced player at a club he's served for most of his adult life.

Decisions have to be taken for the benefit of the majority, not of the few. But those who do take the management route need to understand the responsibility they have for the careers and lives of others.

And Smith didn't.

After twenty years as a pro I was told by letter that I was out of work.

He didn't even have the decency to tell me face to face. I received a letter from the club secretary and that was that.

13

JOURNEYING
1996

THE TREATMENT I RECEIVED from Alan Smith was shoddy to say the least. I'd been a professional for two decades and whatever he thought of me as a player or person, I deserved better.

On the plus side I was confident that I'd soon be with another club, though I was realistic enough to know that it was unlikely to be in the full-time professional ranks.

When I was shipped out to Torquay I was approached by Woking, who were then one of the leading lights in the Conference. Their assistant manager came to see me play a number of times for Wycombe reserves when my loan period ran out in Devon and I was assured they'd be interested in signing me when I became available.

Sure enough, within a few days of me being released by Wycombe, Jeff Chapple, Woking's manager, gave me a call.

"Still interested, Simon?"

I really didn't need much persuading. Woking was a first-class set-up, they were one of the top clubs outside the League, boasted a number of England semi-pro internationals and Clive Walker, who was even older than me, was their star striker. From a playing perspective I was unlikely to get a better offer.

The deal wasn't bad. They were prepared to pay me £300 a week and with no other skills to my name I was hardly in a position to turn down the money. It wasn't a fortune but it was better than signing-on and I could live on that amount.

All seemed fine to start with. I felt fit and strong and I was performing well in training. The only trouble was that I wasn't getting a game and I was only making the substitutes' bench. A few weeks earlier they'd been desperate to sign me. Now I was being called into the manager's office. I was fairly confident it wasn't going to be the offer of a pay rise or an invitation to dinner. And I was right.

"I want to pay you off."

I had to think quickly. They owed me around £9,000 on the balance of my contract and if I took it I'd be free to find another club. Given that I'd not kicked a ball for Woking it would make good sense for me to take the money.

"I understand."

"We're prepared to pay you £4,500."

Now hold on a minute. This wasn't right. Woking had approached me and I had done all I could to prove myself. I was convinced I could have done a job if only Jeff would give me a chance. If they'd got their sums wrong and couldn't afford me then it wasn't my fault. I was having none of it and I told him so.

Eventually a deal was worked out and I was loaned to Walton and Hersham, who were then in Division One of the Ryman League, two steps down the ladder from Woking. Woking would pay half my wages with Walton and Hersham making up the difference.

I can't deny that my pride was hurt. Just over a year previously there had been the possibility, if we'd achieved promotion again, of playing out my days in the First Division with Wycombe. Still, I trained with Dave Russell's side and thoroughly enjoyed it. On my debut in November I played well and scored. The standard might not have been great, but I was back in the game.

In the bar afterwards I requested permission to miss training the following week because I had to visit Blackburn to discuss my ongoing divorce proceedings.

"No problem, Simon, I'll see you on Saturday for the game."

If only.

14

TIME-SERVING
1996

THE MINUTE I MOVED to West Brom my marriage was doomed. A great drinking crowd and a couple of nights a week away from home - life was good. Then when Keith Burkinshaw made it clear I wasn't going to figure in his first team plans it really started to crumble.

The reserves played mid-week, usually Wednesdays, but I still had to be around in case I got called up for the Saturday. Two nights away turned into two nights at home. Mandy asked me to find another club, preferably one closer to home.

I remember the conversation well.

"I've been offered a new club."

"Where?"

"Wycombe."

"Where's that?"

"About a hundred miles south of Birmingham."

Silence. Then the look. Then the words. Then the screams. Then there was no turning back. Then there was no marriage. Then the divorce case started.

Everything was fine to start with, genuinely fine. It was for the best - for us, for the boys. It was over.

She had a solicitor, I had a solicitor, and I was told it would take at least five years to sort the divorce out. I thought that was ridiculous but what could I do?

THERE'S ONLY ONE SIMON GARNER

After a couple of years we didn't appear to be getting anywhere and I knew something had to change. I had to meet with Mandy and her solicitor once every two or three months in Blackburn at the County Court. We'd sit there - me and Mandy, our respective legal advisors and a district judge - in a small upstairs room around a table for an hour and talk about sod-all. It was costing me a fortune so I decided to look after my own affairs which, in hindsight, probably wasn't the most brilliant idea I ever had.

Now I was on my own and I really couldn't see any difference in the proceedings, except my pocket wasn't quite so light every time I left Blackburn. Another five or six times we went through the process - I'd drive the four hours to Blackburn from Berkshire, park on the multi-storey car park near the court, pass the time of day with the security guard, head up the stairs to the room with the table, talk for an hour, go home. Everything was fine, if you count wasting time, effort and money as fine. We'd talk about the kinds of thing you'd expect - how much maintenance I was going to pay, what I'd pay for on top of that. The kinds of things, in fact, two adults who've known each other for a decade and a half should be able to discuss without a bunch of strangers helping you out. But that's divorce for you.

When we first split up I was paying all Mandy's bills at the house in Blackburn and, while we weren't getting on, I didn't mind. Money has never been the greatest motivator for me, I've always been happy to get by with the basic essentials - bed, food, beer, fags.

I was paying about £500 a month in bills, plus the mortgage and whatever the kids wanted. And that was before my own living expenses in Birmingham which, given the amount of partying, were quite substantial. While I was at the peak of my earnings at this time, it was only £600 a week. I use the word 'only' with some trepidation because I think anyone would swap their job, however much they were earning, for mine at that point - playing football with some great players in a very exciting team was magnificent. At the same time, just three or four years later, players in my position were being paid five or ten times that amount.

And so it went on - and I never missed a payment. I had no reason to suspect that my visit north in November 1996 would be any different. I stayed at a friend's the night before but otherwise followed the usual routine: parked on the multi-storey, walked down the steps on to King William Street, took a look in the window at Marks and Spencer then slipped round the side of BHS and into the court building.

"Alright Simon?"

"Fine thanks."

And I was. It had been a good drive up, I was getting a run-out with Walton and Hersham - on a decent whack - and I only had to train twice a week. All was well with the world.

Then the security guard said something I'll never forget. Not that it was anything special, far from it. It was mundane, but it was unexpected, though it didn't register until much later that it had any significance at all.

"You're downstairs today."

No big deal. I'd been going to the court every couple of months for just over two years, every time in the same room, and I thought nothing of the change of location. But as soon as I walked through the door I knew something was going on.

Instead of walking into a small room, maybe 12ft square, with just a single table in it, I was confronted by a whole mass of new faces. There was a woman sitting at a desk with her fingers hovering over a machine like you see on Petrocelli or something; another woman was doing something or other; Mandy was sitting with her solicitor and now a barrister as well. At the back of the court there was Mandy's mum (I do hope Mary found somewhere to park the broomstick) and two smartly-dressed blokes. Smartly-dressed and identically-dressed - definitely not police, definitely not security - though I didn't give them a second thought. Why should I? I'd never been in trouble, never had any contact at all with the police, I didn't know how courts worked. My only experiences with court were the visits to the small upstairs room with the table. I just had this feeling, and it started nagging me.

In reality, the feeling probably came later when I'd had the chance to think about the day; the security guard telling me about the change of room, the new faces in court, the smartly, identically-dressed men.

I was sitting five yards away from Mandy and then I remember somebody, the clerk presumably, saying: "All rise," and I thought, hang on a minute, this ain't right, we're not sitting round doing the usual.

Mandy's barrister called me into the witness box.

"Are you Simon Garner of 7, Bridge Court, Maidenhead."

"No, it's Simon Garner of 1, The High Street, Bray."

A pause.

"Have you disposed of certain monies?"

"Yes. Yes I have."

In 1994 I received a lump sum from the PFA. At thirty-five, that's what happens and in my case I got £25,000. Mandy asked for - and got - an injunction on me spending the money. Fair enough, it was going to form part of the divorce settlement.

A year after I received the money I rang the court at Blackburn. I had a simple request. I wanted to know if the injunction still stood and could I spend any of the money yet. I was told, quite clearly, that the injunction was spent and, yes, I could now access the cash. I've never been one for tidying up the details and I know now I should have had this in writing, but there was a shiny Vauxhall Calibra sitting on Bob Dickinson's forecourt, begging me to buy it. So I did. It was the first new car I'd had in years. When I say new, I don't exactly mean brand new - the Walker revolution came too late for me to properly benefit. I'd asked Bob, a mate, to keep his eyes open for a car for me and he found the Calibra. It cost me nine-and-a-half grand. I only recently got rid of it. It was knackered.

I also paid off some debts, but these weren't gambling debts like one of the papers said, just credit cards. Gambling was never really my scene - beer and cigarettes were my vices. Playing a few hands of cards on the team bus was about as far as it ever got for me and I'd never lose more than £20 in a session.

The barrister carried on his questions, the judge asked a few more, all connected with money. Basically they were asking: "What have you done with the money?" I told them what I'd done, what I'd spent the money on and about my understanding of the injunction, but it transpired I'd been given the wrong information. The injunction still stood. Why I'd been told differently, I just can't say.

More sinister was some questioning about where I was living, which had caused the confusion when I first went into the witness box. I learned that Mandy had put a private detective on my trail while I was living in the south. A private detective! Me! All she had to do to see I'd spent the money was look at the car when I came to see the boys. Except it wasn't quite that simple. According to the dick I lived in a flat - he called on me at Bridge Court - which had a security entrance with a keypad to get in. Frankly, this was bullshit. The detective, by the way, produced no photographs of this supposedly high-class place I was meant to be living in - his word, it seems, was better than mine. I was actually living with my then girlfriend, Heather Kidd, but not on a permanent basis; half the time I was living with my car dealer mate Paddy McClure who lived in Bray. The questions continued for a while and I answered as best I could. I told the truth. I saw no reason to do otherwise. After retiring for a short time, the judge came back into the room.

"Please stand, Mr Garner."

The judge looked up.

"On the evidence presented, Mr Garner, I find you in contempt of court."

I'm not entirely sure what he meant by that. But it was a damned sight easier to understand than what he said next.

"I am, therefore, sentencing you to nine months in prison."

The words echoed round my head. I felt dizzy and sick. My knees went weak. The judge walked out of the room. Mandy ran out of the room. Her mother chased her. I lost all sense of time and space. The room was hazy. I needed a fag.

I had absolutely no idea it was coming. All I expected was to go to the room at the top of the building and have the usual chat. Now I was being told I was going to prison. By the time my head stopped spinning, probably no more than a minute at most, the room was empty except for the woman who had been typing and the two guys in the uniforms which I now recognised for what they were. I sipped on some water - my mouth was so dry. I was shattered.

And then a thought hit me:

How much is my fucking car park bill going to be in nine months?

TIME-SERVING

As far as I knew I'd done nothing wrong. I'd never missed any payments, I'd always arrived at court on time. The contempt was based on the private detective's report saying I lied about where I lived (which I hadn't) and breaking the injunction on spending the money (which I had). Whatever the whys and wherefores, I was now in trouble. Big, big trouble.

There was a lot spinning round my head, but all that would come into focus was the bloody car. That's what landed me in this mess in the first place and, if I didn't do something quickly, it would land me with a bloody great parking fine. So I thought I'd better nip out and move it.

"OK if I nip out and move the car? It's on the multi-storey and I don't want nine months' worth of parking tickets on it when I get out."

Not surprisingly, the question was ignored.

"If you'll come with us downstairs, Mr Garner."

Well, I've seen it on the telly. From Kojak to The Bill I know you can at least make a phone call.

"Can I make a phone call?"

"No."

This was getting silly. I've spent my whole adult life being kicked from every angle and relishing the challenge of getting back up and back to it, but this was different; the rules had changed, I couldn't kick back. So I asked nicely.

"Look, please, I've got my mobile with me. Do you mind if I just make a couple of calls."

In all my time as a footballer I've had one freebie. It was the night I scored five against Derby and I was at a pub on the outskirts of Blackburn, The Bull's Head, for something to eat after celebrating down at the 100 Club earlier. After the meal I asked for the bill.

"Simon, it's on me - great game today."

I felt something between embarrassment and pride and accepted the gesture with genuine appreciation.

"We really aren't supposed to do this, Simon, but we know who you are. Go on, make your calls."

This, the second freebie, was a long time coming but I was no less chuffed.

First on my calling list was Heather, who I'd left the night before saying I'd be back for tea-time. I got through first time.

"I've got us lasagne, what time will you be home?"

She didn't find it funny when I said August. Those were not tears of joy.

Bob Dickinson was next. I'd stayed with him the previous night and we'd had a great time.

"Enjoy that pint, Simon, you might be going to prison tomorrow!"

We laughed.

"Piss off!"

We laughed some more. Ho ho.

It was Bob, you'll remember, who sold me the bloody car which started all this.

"Look, Bob, my car's on the car park, can you come and get it?"

"Why?"

"Because I'm going to prison."

"Yeah, right."

I wanted to flatten him.

"Bob, this is serious. I'm going down for nine months. The battery's running out on my mobile and I am not joking. My car's on the car park. It's on level 1. I'll leave the keys here. Go and get the car. I can't afford a bloody parking ticket."

TIME-SERVING

He got the message and just in time because the phone then went dead. I sat drinking coffee, smoking my last fag of freedom and tried to get my head round what was happening. Shit, I didn't even have a lawyer.

"Ready?"

"What for?"

"We're going now."

"Going where?"

"We're going to Preston jail."

It really hadn't sunk in. Having a pair of cuffs clamped round my wrists soon sorted that out. But it was still difficult to comprehend. I'd never been in trouble with the police, never broken the law. I didn't have some Swiss bank account where I'd stashed my millions from football. I wasn't exactly what you'd call a rich man. Never have been. Never will be. But I doubt if that's the way people at that time were viewing footballers.

Blackburn Rovers had recently won the championship with a team including two British record signings - Alan Shearer and Chris Sutton - who were earning a fortune. By association, and as a former fans' favourite, people probably thought I earned a fortune too and that I was up to something devious. I know some thought I was being done for not looking after the kids properly or evading tax - but it was much simpler than that. I had made a mistake and I didn't even know I'd made it. And my sentence was harsher than for most burglars. That's justice for you.

In the room below the court the two prison officers told me not to worry, that I'd be out in four months. Some comfort. It was November 18, less than a week to my birthday. My kids had birthdays coming up and it was just five weeks to Christmas. I was going to be in jail at Christmas. And I was wearing handcuffs.

THERE'S ONLY ONE SIMON GARNER

I got into the back of a Volvo with absolutely no idea what was going on, we drove to Preston nick - about a twenty minute journey - and ended up in a waiting-room at the prison. There were bars on the windows.

A guard looked at me.

"What are you doing here Simon?"

"I don't bloody know. I haven't a clue."

I was in a state of shock with just six fags in my pocket. I knew I should have asked them to stop on the way.

I waited for an hour on my own. It was the pits, like sitting in a toilet without the smell - or at least without the smell of a toilet. The smell of 'institution' was there though - stale bodies, stale food, stale cheap tobacco.

Now I'm quite happy getting naked in the company of men, it goes with the job. But I didn't feel so comfortable doing it in a prison. I stripped off and was given a set of prison overalls - very fetching - and they took everything off me except the cigarettes. The lighter went though.

Another waiting-room, this one with a grubby bunch of blokes, and I sat there for two hours. It was eerie, the conversation revolving only around whether anyone had any fags. I kept quiet, I only had half a dozen - certainly not enough to share with twenty or so blokes who, quite frankly, looked like criminals. I wondered which one of these gentleman I'd be sharing a cell with.

Eventually a warder arrived and started directing these guys, whose only other discernible physical attributes ranged from mean-looking to tough-looking. And covered in tattoos. More worrying, they seemed perfectly at ease in their surroundings.

The only exceptions were me and a bloke in the corner who was in for drink-driving. We looked as mean and tough as laboratory mice. And we were just as scared.

People kept walking in, prisoners who'd just been sent down.

"Alright mate, what are you in for this time?"

It was like a youth club for hard nuts. Still, at least I got to share a cell with Mr DD, or Alan from Blackpool as he introduced himself - it was his third conviction for the same offence. Pillock.

Bunk bed, toilet (flushable), sink, table, barred window, cream walls, six by ten. It's amazing the detail you can pick up when there's so few distractions. Within a minute of me stepping into the room, there's a knock at the door.

"You all right in there? Do you want anything?"

I thought it was a warder. It wasn't. It was Dunc.

"Are you all right, son?"

"No, not really."

"What do you need?"

"I need a pillow and I could do with some matches."

Five minutes later I had a pillow and a box of matches. Another half hour passed and this time it was a warder at the door.

"Garner?"

"Yes, that's me."

"If you're thinking of appealing, you need to fill in this form."

Appeal? Of course I'm going to bloody appeal. He also told me there'd been a call from a firm in Manchester, George Davis & Co, who work on behalf of the PFA and had promised a solicitor would be with me the next day.

I hardly slept at all. Neither of us did. It just kept spinning round my head - what the hell am I doing here, this isn't right. Looking back I wondered why I wasn't scared, but Dunc's visit made me feel quite strong. I was known, I was a personality of sorts, I'd be alright.

THERE'S ONLY ONE SIMON GARNER

The next morning, after breakfast, I got the message I was moving on to Kirkham open prison. Cuffs on again - as if I was going to do a runner, the warders clearly didn't know my current state of fitness - and into the back of a black moria.

"You get your kit from over there and then they'll tell you which hut you're going in."

Kirkham's an old RAF camp - long huts, flat landscape and about as inviting as cold porridge. Which is appropriate.

The regime, as well as the surroundings, was very different to my brief experience of Preston. There's eight or ten rooms to a hut - cells would be the wrong word because you're not locked in - a television room, showers, a bath.

"You're in B2. Find a bed."

Out of all the rooms in B2 hut there were just two beds left. In one I could see all manner of pictures and paraphernalia about Liverpool Football Club. In the other room, all I could see were pictures of topless birds. I didn't want to see his paraphernalia, so went for the scouse football fan. At least we'd have something to talk about. I made my bed up. Then started to feel isolated. Something'll happen, I was thinking. I'm going home in a minute. All of a sudden this huge geezer walked into the room. Big, black, built like a breezeblock shithouse, mid-twenties. Scary.

"Alright?" I said. He looked at me then turned round and blanked me completely, never said a word. Double scary.

"Hello, I'm Simon. How are you?"

He was silent. Then I saw the scar on his face - from chin to forehead. Scary no longer seemed a strong enough word.

He was messing about in a drawer at the end of his bed then stopped abruptly. He turned, stood up, and stared down at me.

"You're Simon Garner, aren't you?"

TIME-SERVING

I looked at his pictures of Liverpool and I thought, shit, I hope he doesn't remember the goals I scored against them.

"Er, yeah."

"Nice one, man. I'm Pete, pleased to meet you."

And, as this great shovel of a hand crushed my fingers, I thought, phew. And so we talked about football, about me scoring against Liverpool, which he thankfully didn't hold against me. But the conversation took an odd turn.

"I've enjoyed talking with you, Simon, but being in here is a bit like playing for a football team."

Eh?

"You can't do it on your own, you need people to help out."

Erm.

"And I'm going to look after you."

Which I have to say, if only for a few seconds as I recalled a couple of jokes about prisons and showers, caused me some concern.

"Whenever you're in this hut, I'm your minder. We have tea at 5.30, we get locked up at . . ."

I breathed a sigh of relief. What a grand lad!

Over tea the prison routine was explained more fully and, if I'm being honest, it wasn't as bad as I'd imagined. There was a lot of freedom of movement and the food was OK.

I do worry about people's perceptions of this more relaxed approach to treating prisoners, and you have to remember that Kirkham was for low-risk inmates only. I know there are many who believe a prison regime should be tough, aggressive even, that prisoners deserve punishment in its bluntest terms. But can you imagine not having easy access to your loved ones, not being able to meet your mates, not being able to go to the match on Saturday or work on Monday? That's the punishment: being, as lawyers like to say, deprived of one's liberty.

THERE'S ONLY ONE SIMON GARNER

A case in point.

"Do you need anything?"

I had cigarettes for now - priority number one sorted, but I needed a phone card. Pete, god bless him, lent me one. And then I went to use it. There was, naturally, a queue, as there was every evening. The phones were turned on at 6 pm and lock-up was at 8.30pm. With queues of up to ninety minutes to use the phone the only way to guarantee making a call is by missing tea. Even if people do hold that prisoners should be punished as well as being kept out of society for a while, does it serve anyone's interests that a dad can't say goodnight to a child because there aren't enough telephones?

We're still, by the way, on my first day at Kirkham, my second of incarceration, and I was really starting to regret my decision to dispense with my lawyer despite the assurance of an imminent visit by a PFA representative.

Pete and I were nattering in the room after tea when - at last - there was a knock on the door at 7.30. But the little lad in the prison garb who poked his head round the door didn't look much of a brief.

"Simon Garner?"

"Yeah?"

"Somebody wants to see you in C2."

"Who?"

"John wants to see you in C2."

The distant tinkle of alarm bells could be heard.

"I don't know any John."

"He wants to see you in C2."

This was now an instruction rather than a request. I lit a cigarette, as much to look hard as to try and calm down, and pointed to Pete.

"Mind if my mate comes along?"

"He's not coming."

"What do you mean?"

"He's not coming."

Then he ran off. And Pete and I carried on talking. Half an hour later he was back.

"Simon, for your own good, come to C2."

The tone was now urgent-approaching-desperate.

"Right. He'll come, but I'm coming too."

Thank you again Pete.

On the end of a bed in a well turned-out room in C2, John was relaxing. I learnt immediately that he came from Blackburn. Seconds later I knew he 'ran' Kirkham Open Prison. I knew it because he told me. Any suspicions he might be winding me up were dismissed almost instantly because he was certainly well-connected.

"I knew you were coming today."

"How did you know?"

"I had a message from Preston nick. They let me know."

I didn't ask, but I'd still like to know who 'they' were. Then he took me by surprise, because up until this point, what with all the trouble it had taken to get me there, it felt like an interrogation or, at best, a job interview.

"What do you need?"

My preconceptions about prison daddies - based only on having seen Ray Winstone wielding a snooker ball-filled sock in the film Scum - were beginning to feel heavy-handed.

"I've got a phone card now but I could do with some tobacco."

"OK."

The lackey produced some.

"You're in B2 aren't you?"

"Yeah."

THERE'S ONLY ONE SIMON GARNER

"Who's looking after you?"

Pete was just out of vision by the door.

"Well, Pete. He's here now. He's looking after me well."

"Good. But from now on Andy is looking after you when you go for a meal. If you're going to the gym Dave looks after you. When you're at work Steve looks after you and when you've got your spare time, if you go to the library or anywhere else, Tony looks after you."

Everywhere I went after that, my team of minders would pop with a 'Hello Simon, everything alright?' I'd never experienced anything like this level of celebrity in football, and it was a weird feeling.

"Hi Simon, I'm Keith - Dave's ill - I'll be with you in the gym."

Bloody hell. A real star at last! All I needed now was a pair of shades and a stretch limo.

I got a real cushy job in the laundry. It helped that the guy who ran it was from Darwen and was a big Blackburn fan. The work was OK but the money was terrible: £4.50 a week. A packet of fags and a £2 phone card and you're into overdraft. And you don't even get paid in cash, it's credited to your account at the tuckshop. Like everyone else, I latched on to the fact you could get 2½ oz of baccy, a phone card and a few teabags for that, so it was bye-bye Silk Cut. All things considering it wasn't turning out to be a bad day. I even got to meet my new solicitor.

Roger Davies was a great bloke and a straight-talker and I immediately felt things were getting sorted out. He was already working on an appeal and suggested I get a barrister. Now I know it was important and I was in jail and desperately needed to get out, but I knew I wouldn't be able to afford the £750 an hour or whatever. Shit, I was on Legal Aid. So I asked Roger to contact a barrister I knew, Stephen Dodds - a mad Blackburn Rovers fan. Stephen's uncle was a really keen fan as well. He died at a game away at Carlisle and his widow presented a trophy to the club, The Arthur Todd Memorial Cup. I was the first winner for the five I scored against Derby and Stephen presented it to me. The first time I met him we talked about football for forty-five minutes and my case for fifteen. We also smoked a pack of twenty between us.

Roger made a number of visits and with every one I felt we were making progress. A couple of weeks into the sentence I bumped into my old mate, the solicitor Paul Schofield, in the visiting room. He was seeing a client and Roger had just left. It was good to see a friendly face.

With what was a strong team working for me, it became easier to settle into the prison routine. No question it was miserable, boring and I missed my children and friends, but I made the best of it and it helped to have people watching out for me, people who'd bring something back from the canteen while I was standing in the phone queue.

And, of course, I got asked to play for the prison football team. I forget who the opposition was, but they were a local team who fancied getting stuck into the lags. We murdered them and I got a double hat-trick, but this central defender just kept taking lumps out of me - partly because I was in prison - and with some added venom because of my Blackburn connections. I asked him as nicely as possible to stop kicking me. No. I threatened him. And it worked to a point. A minute later he flattened one of my team-mates who, not having had the benefit of my grammar school education, took a more direct course of action to prevent further hassle and punched him square in the face. This was not handbags at ten paces and a few more got involved.

THERE'S ONLY ONE SIMON GARNER

At right-back we had one of three warders in the team. He came running across and I thought there might be some trouble. There was. He twatted the opposition defender who started it.

My professional income might have dried up, but I got an ounce of baccy for being man-of-the-match which, in prison, is more useful than a substantial win-bonus on the outside.

It was the done thing to call the warders 'screws', but I tried not to. It wasn't me at all and, with one exception, I got on well with them. He was just a tiresome dickhead and I did wonder for a while if he was a Burnley fan. I was treated well by inmates and staff everywhere, but this guy seemed to go out of his way to wind people up. If you got a visit on a Sunday, you had to wait in the recreation room for your name to be shouted.

"Garner, you little shit, your visit's here."

OK, so it was hardly grand-scale abuse, but it was unnecessary and provocative.

Some days later, after more legal discussions, I was chatting to Pete in the room. There was a calendar behind him.

"That's when I'm going - the 17th December."

"No way. You got nine months, you'll be here until April."

We were both wrong, but I was less wrong. On the afternoon of the 17th one of the warders came in.

"Garner?"

"Yes"

"2136?"

"Yes."

"Be ready at half past nine tomorrow morning. You're going back to Preston."

I'd been given no notice at all, but it looked liked the appeal was moving ahead. A miserable night was spent on the drugs wing at Preston - I have no idea why the drugs wing was chosen, perhaps because there wasn't a six pints of mild and 20 Silk Cut wing. I was in the company of Space Cadet Mick and a father and son burglary team from Darwen who, through a relative who worked at some law firm in Blackburn, heard I was being transferred back to Preston. They'd come to look after me. What a friendly place prison is!

Handcuffs back on and another ride in a black moria for the journey back to Blackburn. It was slow and bumpy and I needed a wee. I saw Stephen in an upstairs room but I was still wearing the cuffs. At least now I wasn't handcuffed to one of the prison officers like I had been in the van. Stephen got his cigarettes out straight away - not only was he a fine lawyer, he was a mind-reader too. I couldn't light the cigarette because of the cuffs and Stephen asked if they could be removed. They couldn't. But I still needed the loo and they still refused to uncuff me. They let me have a little privacy, by tying a chain to the cuffs so I couldn't run off. Public enemy number one, Mr Simon Garner.

Stephen and I talked through the proceedings and then we were back into the same courtroom I'd last seen a month ago. And - unbelievable - in front of the same judge. My hands were still cuffed and now I was chained to each of the prison officers who flanked me. No defender had ever been so close.

It seemed like an eternity, but it probably only took fifteen minutes for Stephen to do his bit.

"Mr Garner would like the court to know how much he regrets his actions and for his contempt of court."

That was the gist of it.

Five minutes later - a bloody long five minutes, mind you - the judge set me free after serving four weeks of a nine month sentence. I sat back down. I couldn't take it in. Only when the prison officers took the cuffs off did I feel like it was happening to me and not someone else. Stephen and I went back to the room upstairs and that's when I realised the press was there. I really didn't want to do it, but Stephen persuaded me to give an interview to the Lancashire Evening Telegraph so I could say thank you to people in Blackburn for their good wishes and letters. I was glad he made me go through with it.

While this was going on Heather had gone to fetch the car and I came out of court with her sister Elizabeth. Unfortunately for Elizabeth, she was pictured in the Telegraph next to a picture of Mandy and was wrongly billed as one of 'The Two Women In Simon Garner's Life'.

I hadn't seen the kids in over a month. We'd written, but it's not the same. Our first stop was St Bede's school. To them it was like nothing had happened. For me it was like everything had. We were together for about fifteen minutes, but they had to get back to lessons. We drove home, back to Berkshire, stopping only for forty Silk Cut. And then I got gloriously drunk on two pints of lager.

15

RETIRING
1997 to 2002

ONCE THE HANGOVER had subsided I had some serious thinking to do. I was now unemployed and, having spent a month in prison with only limited opportunities to keep myself fit, I was hardly going to be at the top of any potential manager's shopping list.

My contract with Woking was terminated during my stay at Her Majesty's pleasure. They wrote and said that since I was unavailable for training I was in breach of my contract. It added insult to the injury of incarceration. I argued that I was hardly in a position to fulfil my duties but it didn't get me far. The PFA, once again, gave me a leg-up when it was most needed and at least managed to secure two weeks' wages. But that wasn't going to last long.

Another letter I received while at Kirkham was from Steve Hayes, a Wycombe fan. It was more positive.

"If you're stuck for work when you get out, give me a call."

I was on the blower within a couple of days and landed myself my first proper job - I was to sell mortgages to people who wanted to buy their council houses. The gesture from Steve was much appreciated, though I didn't really enjoy the work. The travelling was dreadful and my area essentially covered the whole of the south - from Birmingham downwards.

There were days when I'd have to drive to Cornwall for an evening appointment and I wouldn't get home until two or three in the morning but still have to be ready the next day for another assignment. While Steve was still with the company I could cope because he made sure my diary didn't clash with football training. But when he left, the writing was on the wall.

It was odd having to wear a suit and tie to work. And I certainly had responsibilities that just didn't exist in sport. As a footballer so much of your life is managed for you. You turn up when you're told to and someone else takes care of the details. At training there are always balls ready to kick and cones to run round. On away trips you arrive at the allotted time and someone takes you to a hotel where the rooms have already been booked and a table reserved for dinner. On match days you get presented with a clean kit and told to get on with the job. Football has its stresses, of course, but on balance they're fairly inconsequential. All you really do is play the game. And once the game's over you've got time to prepare for the next one. Real jobs aren't like that.

Steve left the firm and then it relocated from Watford to Wolverhampton and I was expected to travel to the Black Country three times a week. No chance, not on the money I was being paid. Don't get me wrong, it was better than being on the dole, but it became a choice between football and the job. Football and secure money, if you like. No contest.

On getting out of prison I decided the only way I was going to get another club was by touting myself around. I contacted the local paper and they printed a story saying I was available. Gordon Bartlett, who was manager at Wealdstone, a Ryman League Division Three outfit, contacted me and offered £70 a game and the promise that the club was going places. Given that both Stuart Pearce and Vinnie Jones had started their careers with the club, it didn't seem a bad offer. It was a very solid outfit and we were promoted at the end of the season.

Just before promotion I handed my notice in with the mortgage company and went straight into a job as a postman, pounding the streets of Maidenhead. The early starts suited my wish to keep playing - I was finished for lunchtime so there was no problem with two nights a week of training. The only difficulty was the fact I had to work on Saturday mornings and by the time it came to kick-off I was already feeling knackered. Add in a few pints after the game and Sundays became totally dedicated to recovery. Mind you, all the walking kept me fit.

I stayed another season with Wealdstone, though part way through I signed briefly for Dagenham and Redbridge who were in the Conference. It was a move I couldn't turn down because it meant playing at a higher level - and my money shot up to £150 a game. The only trouble was that after a couple of training sessions and half a game I was told that, after all, I wasn't really the type of player they wanted.

No big deal. I rang Gordon and he immediately offered me the chance to go back to Wealdstone.

It was to be a year of some turmoil for me. If you tot it all up I had three football clubs, three jobs, three homes and two girlfriends. Still, it kept me from being bored.

Heather and I split up at the end of the season and the only number Gordon had for me was Heather's. I'm not the best at keeping in touch and when Windsor and Eton found me I took them up on the offer of playing for them in Ryman League Division Two.

Less satisfactory was the fact I was living in a bedsit after moving out of Heather's. I hated it, but I wasn't there long. I went to a party with my mate Paddy McClure and met Suzy.

We clicked instantly and soon I moved into her house at Cookham in Berkshire. We married the following year, in April 1999. She must be special, because I've even managed to give up smoking since being with her.

I gave up the post job when another pal, Billy Simons, offered me a job as a painter and decorator, something I kept up with until the autumn of 2001. That August Suzy gave birth to Thomas William and after her maternity leave was finished she went back to work and I became a house husband. It made sense for a number of reasons with the main one being that Suzy's earning potential in the marketing world was a damn sight better than mine in the home decoration business!

I didn't mind the decorating and always had a laugh with the lads I worked with. We once had a job at Ed de Goey's house near Windsor. He had no idea who I was, of course, so I told him. I don't think he was particularly impressed.

Just before Thomas was born Windsor and Eton's manager, Alan Davies, moved on and the new boss - I hope this isn't getting boring - didn't much like the look of me either, so I signed for Flackwell Heath, a division below, for the 1999-2000 season.

Playing for fun and expenses I had a great time. The club was just five minutes' drive from home and the lads in the side were enthusiastic about the game. I couldn't have asked for much more in my last season.

But the years were catching up with me. My ankles and knees were starting to cause me real problems. They'd had enough and, frankly, so had the rest of me. I couldn't train any more because my body wouldn't allow more than one rigorous work-out each week. The morning after a game I was aching all over. Ultimately, it wasn't a difficult decision.

RETIRING

I thought about it for a couple of weeks and then walked away. The only trouble was, I couldn't completely leave football behind. I wanted to be involved in some way but not in a playing capacity, or serious playing capacity, and certainly not on the coaching or management side.

When Wycombe offered me the chance to do some match-day public relations work I jumped at the chance and for a season I kept corporate guests entertained with stories from the past.

But I was getting more enjoyment from media work. My friendship with Alan Parry led to me performing the analyst's role on Sky Sports when they had the contract for the Nationwide League, and I started working regularly for BBC Radio Lancashire on Blackburn games when they were in the south. I'm also regularly called on by the national and regional media to talk about the prospects of my former clubs.

Doing the PR work for Wycombe also gave me the confidence to start working on sportsmen's dinners, first as an MC and then as a main speaker.

But my main job now is looking after Thomas and I take a great deal of pleasure from that. It's like going back in time to when John and James were little and I used to take them on long walks round Blackburn. The key difference is that Cookham is very flat and that suits my knees much better.

As for playing, I have a mid-week five-a-side run-out with friends and I play for Blackburn Rovers veterans once in a while. I was in the team over the summer of 2002 that played at the MEN Arena in the tournament that was beamed live on Sky Sports. It was the best pay-day from football I'd ever had. I hope soon to turn out one last time in the blue and white halves at Ewood Park. When I left the club I was promised a benefit game and I'd like to take up the offer.

THERE'S ONLY ONE SIMON GARNER

I still get down to Wycombe on a regular basis and I have a lot of friends there. I also try to get to Ewood Park when I'm visiting my sons and I always get a great reception from the supporters and officials. Before the 5-0 drubbing of Burnley in 2001 I was asked to give an interview to the club's television station but it had to be conducted in the tunnel and not on the pitch. I think they were concerned my presence would inflame the visiting supporters. At least, I hope that's what they were thinking!

I doubt if anyone heard a word of the interview though, because as it was shown on the screen the chant was deafening - 'There's Only One Simon Garner'. It sounded as good as it ever did.

When I started out I had three ambitions. I wanted to break records, I wanted to play at Wembley and I wanted to perform in the top flight.

I achieved the first two. I might have achieved the third as well if I'd taken Kenny's offer of being a squad player after promotion in 1992, but I doubt it. There were too many good strikers ahead of me to even be sure of getting on the bench.

But I don't regret the decision to move on. In the end the ambition changed. I simply wanted to play the game. There is only one Simon Garner, and that Simon Garner is a footballer.